*Humor is the great thing - the saving thing after all.  The minute it crops up all our hardnesses yield, all our irritations and resentments slip away and a sunny spirit takes their place.*   - Mark Twain

# RUFF TALES

## HIGH OCTANE STORIES
## FROM THE
## RUFF CREEK GENERAL STORE

### Retold by

# Joe McHugh

### Illustrated by

## Paula Blasius

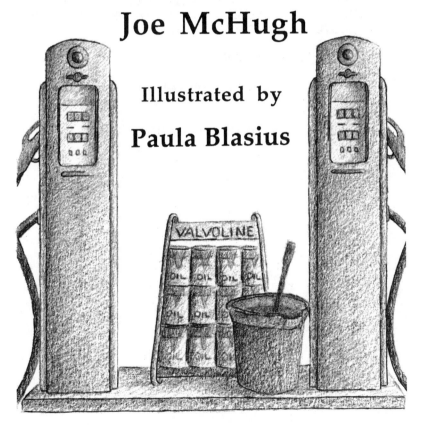

*Catalpa Press*
P.O. Box 7468
Auburn, CA 95604

This book is dedicated to my family,
they know who they are.

## *Acknowledgements*

I would like to thank all those generous souls who helped bring these stories to print. These include Dan and Barbara Morris, Ray and Karen Stockdale, Tom Freyvogel, Jake Mankey, Wayne Miller, Kissy Davin, Michael Chirigos, Jim Nedresky, Robin Moore, and the faculty and students of Waynesburg College.
I am particularly grateful to my mother, Beverly Quinn McHugh, for her invaluable contribution as editor and source of inspiration.
Lastly, I wish to acknowledge the debt I owe the many fine storytellers I have met over the years who have taken the time to share their stories with me.

# *Contents*

## *Preface*

For a number of years I have made my living as a professional storyteller and traditional musician, performing at schools, museums, grange halls, libraries, and festivals throughout the United States. In 1984 I moved my family from West Virginia to Greene County, Pennsylvania, purchasing a small farm near Waynesburg. My father's people were from southwestern Pennsylvania and it's been a great pleasure to me to walk the same hills as they did when first they arrived in America from Ireland. As I often perform in the Pittsburgh area I must drive over the ridge to Ruff Creek to get on Interstate 79. I've gotten in the habit of stopping at the Ruff Creek General Store to buy my gas and indulge in a Dole frozen-fruit bar.

Ray Stockdale and his wife, Karen, are the owners of the store. Ray loves to hear and tell jokes and, as that's my passion as well, we have swapped many good stories over the years. Most of Ray's collection of anecdotes and tall tales he's picked up from his regular customers, like Kissy Davin and Wayne Miller, who are natural-born storytellers in their own right. For my own part, the stories I've told in return are those I've gleaned from numerous years of living in the central Appalachians, an area rich in oral literature. These are stories I have often performed and have found them to be popular with both urban and rural audiences of all ages.

Recently my family, along with my partner and illustrator, Paula Blasius, decided to relocate to another part of the country. I know I shall miss the relaxed, enjoyable moments I have spent sharing stories with Ray and the others down at the store. I've decided to write this book, before we leave, to serve as a record of these tales and perhaps, more importantly, to reflect the simple human warmth and wisdom I found there.

I make no claim upon the "originality" of these stories. It is said that if Adam and Eve ever return to the earth, the only thing they'll recognize are the old stories. They are part of our heritage as Americans, faithfully passed from one generation to the next. They belong to everyone, I merely borrow a few.

On the other hand, I am not a folklorist, and it is not my intention to scientifically document the folktales of the Appalachians. With generous use of my imagination, and, I trust, respect for the tradition, I have reworked, modified, and embellished many of these tales as plot and circumstance seemed to warrant. I offer them for simple enjoyment since it was with this intent that they were first told to me. Furthermore, I consider the fine people of Greene County to be friends and would not, for the world, insult or embarrass anyone. All but a few of the names, therefore, are fictitious and bear no resemblance to anyone living or dead.

Although I have attempted to set these tales down on paper in a way that best expresses the wonderful mountain style in which they are told, they remain essentially spoken stories. They are never told the same way twice and will often involve the listener in some way in the telling. This spontaneous and participatory quality acts to keep the tales continually fresh and satisfying. The greatest compliment you could give this author is to read the stories in this book and then go out and tell them.

Joe McHugh, the Mayor of Mudlick, 1988

# Introduction

This book is about an old-fashioned general store and the art of storytelling. It is full of light-hearted yarns and colorful characters. There are stories about city-slickers and country-wits, (called "hill-hoppers and stump-jumpers in Ruff Creek), stubborn mules, three-legged chickens, haunted coal mines, and frustrated ministers. Although located in western Pennsylvania, the stories themselves are universal. They are an integral part of America's rich oral literature and, as such, could be as easily heard in a country store in the bayous of Louisiana, the lake country of Wisconsin, the granite hills of Vermont, or the coastal forests of Oregon.

## The Store

If you happen to be traveling down Interstate 79 through the rugged hills of Greene County in southwestern Pennsylvania, just before crossing the border into West Virginia, you'll see a sign for Ruff Creek. Slow down and take the exit. The village of Ruff Creek is not much more than a crossroads where Rt. 221 intersects Rt. 19. There's a red-brick Baptist church with an old-fashioned hillside cemetery, a barber shop, a video-rental business built on the back of someone's house, the township building, a garage for repairing everything from diesel trucks to lawn mowers, and the general store.

Except for the gas pumps out front and an odd assortment of signs, the Ruff Creek General Store looks more like a house than a place of business. Long a fixture in Greene County, it is a "general" store in the truest sense of the word, selling a wide variety of merchandise from groceries, clothing, and footware to hardware, feed, and kerosene. The current owners are Ray and Karen Stockdale. Ray, a graduate of West Virginia University, took the store over from his father, Jack, when he retired. Despite the long hours and lack of big city amenities, the Stockdales are proud of their store and the important role it plays in the community.

In an age of television and mass-marketing, where "image" is everything, (and content often sadly neglected), the general store is refreshingly simple and direct. It is exactly what it presents itself to be. What it sells is displayed without pretense or artifice. Prices, although often a few cents higher than in the chain stores, are plainly marked on items and are not figured by a computer. Customers are known on a first-name basis and their trade is appreciated. No matter how much or how little money people spend in the store, they are treated with the same courtesy and friendliness.

It doesn't take long, sitting on the bench in the store and observing the daily activity, the comings and goings, to realize that the store is not only the economic center of this small farming and coal mining community, it is also its social and cultural center as well.

Ray, and the others who work at the store, informally carry out the essential function of disseminating a wide range of necessary information to the people of the area. The bulletin board, back by the meat counter, is a convenient place to give away puppies, rent a house, learn about the next church social, or sell property. The store is also the place where many of Ruff Creek's young people work their first job and where a customer can get a check cashed easily. And, lastly, there's the storytelling.

It is perhaps a fortunate coincidence that the word "store" and the word "story" are so very close, for in no other place but a country store is one as likely to hear a well-told story. They go together so naturally that one, without the other, is unimaginable. Why is it then that the country store is so well suited to this enjoyable activity? There are several basic reasons. For one, the general store, viewed as a sort of stage, is hard to surpass. All day long it is frequented by a diverse and engaging assortment of local residents. Chance meetings are commonplace and lend themselves to the spontaneous swapping of tales and good-natured competition. There is a rich texture of history at the store in everything from the simple, functional architecture and worn oak floors to the old-fashioned pressed-tin ceiling. The air is a mixture of wonderful aromas, fresh-brewed coffee, cheeses, and sweet molasses. The atmosphere is friendly and unhurried, an inviting place to linger awhile away from the cares and stress of a busy world. Here is a physical and social environment in harmony with the intimate nature of storytelling.

Another essential aspect of the store's role as a place of storytelling is its rural location. Storytelling relies for its effectiveness primarily on action, humor, and unusual or unexpected occurrences. Country life provides an abundance of this raw material. A teacher in Greene County, who sold his 35 acre farm and moved to Waynesburg, was eventually reprimanded by his fellow teachers in Pittsburgh. They said that since his move to town he no longer had any good stories to tell. He sadly realized that they were right. Instead of

8

risking life and limb repairing a roof in a thunder storm, finding an abandoned fawn along the road, or having the tractor brakes fail on a steep hill while taking the relatives for a hayride, he now stayed in the house and watched other peoples' made-up adventures on the video player.

Country people often possess an appreciation of language itself, not just as a means of conveying facts, but for the sheer pleasure of it. Attention is paid to the sound of the human voice, its variety and texture. There is a rich, imaginative use of similes. In the humorous anecdote, or joke, the enjoyment is in the story itself. The punch-line, although carefully crafted to fetch a laugh, serves more as a destination, the journey being the real purpose.

Finally, the store's real virtue as a home for storytelling is its interrelatedness to the stuff of everyday life. In more urbanized areas, retired men who spend their time in the indoor malls seem seldom to tell stories. Little in the shiny, high-tech environment around them has to do with their own lives, either past or present. The country store, on the other hand, is full of familiar things that relate directly to the lives and work of the people who shop there. A farmer feels naturally at ease sitting next to a bin of fencing staples or sacks of calf-starter. It's not much different from sitting in his own barn or workshed. There he is usually alone, a good thing if his work requires individual attention, but at the store, he's in the company of neighbors, a good thing for telling a story.

## The Storytellers

*"To be a good storyteller one must be gloriously alive. It is not possible to kindle fresh fires from burned-out embers."* - *Ruth Sawyer*

The art of storytelling is an ancient one. Since the invention of language itself, storytellers have been society's entertainers, social critics, journalists, and teachers. Whether Hassidic rabbi, Cheyenne medicine-man, or Irish bard, the tellers are the faithful custodians of an important part of the cultural heritage left by those who have passed this way before. No mere historians, they are creative artists in their own right, tapping the multi-faceted vein of imagination deep within the human psyche to discover new meaning in the irony and paradoxes of life.

The mountain storytellers of western Pennsylvania and West Virginia are a vital part of this noble tradition. Uniquely American, they intuitively understand the value of folk stories and keep them alive with both humor and style. Truth, in a limited sense, is not their concern, (lawyers and preachers, the professional purveyors of truth in society, are the butt of much of their ridicule). They are more interested in *insight*, that momentary glimpse of the "bigger picture" that is often found in the ordinary affairs of day-to-day life and the unexpected heart-felt laugh. They poke fun at the self-important, invent strange and fantastic creatures, laugh at life's small humiliations, and help reawaken a sense of mystery and wonder in existence itself. Without them, and their lively imaginations and vitality, the world can be a dreary and prosaic affair.

## The Tales

The stories presented in this book cover a wide range of story types most commonly found in the American oral tradition. They have been organized into seven chapters with the first, <u>Around the Store</u>, serving to introduce the reader to both the store and its main characters. <u>Country Wit and Wisdom</u> is one of the larger chapters since rural people, often at a disadvantage both financially and politically, place great value upon these virtues. While they take delight in outsmarting the city-slicker, they derive equal pleasure from getting the upper-hand of a neighbor, as is evident in the Charlie and Oscar tales.

A collection of exaggerated stories is found in the next chapter, <u>The Taller The Better.</u> Although found in European culture, most notably the Baron Munchausen tales, the tall tale truly came into its own in America. To be most effective, the tall tale must attend scrupulously to every detail, going to extremes at times to uphold the strictest accuracy. But then, when the end is reached, it becomes completely preposterous. This contrast is the source of its humor. <u>Dogs, Horses, and Mules</u> brings together several light-hearted stories about the four-legged creatures most closely associated with rural life. The chapter on <u>Kissy Davin</u> presents a number of imaginative tall tales and anecdotes typical of the mountain storyteller. <u>Mountain Humor</u> is an assortment of old and new jokes that could be heard any day down at the general store. <u>Touch of the Supernatural</u> presents three tradtional ghost stories and a devil tale that challenge our notions of the world of the unseen. Finally, the book closes on a lighter note with the chapter, <u>At the Gates of Heaven</u>.

# CHAPTER ONE

# Around the Store

*You can learn much in a country store*
- P.T. Barnum

# High Water

In late November of 1985, Greene County experienced some disastrous flooding after several days and nights of drenching rain. Many of the creeks overflowed their banks and, in some places, the waters covered the roads, making travel impossible. The area around Ruff Creek was particularly hard hit. The general store lost a great deal of merchandise to water damage when its basement was flooded. Worst of all, the underground gas storage tanks were also ruined and had to be replaced at considerable cost. It was some time until the store was back to normal.

Now not far from the general store, an old farmhouse had a rough time of it. It was completely surrounded by brown swirling water. Two young boys were upstairs in the house looking out of the window and enjoying themselves. As with most kids, the flood was an adventure. They excitedly watched as bits of old furniture, broken tree limbs, and even a neighbor's chicken coop floated past. The boys then noticed an old straw hat go by. They didn't pay much attention to it at first, until it got just below the house. Then, it suddenly changed direction and began floating back the way it had come, against the current. The puzzled boys watched as the hat reached the other end of the house, where it again reversed itself, and once more floated down with the water. This went on five or six times, the hat going back and forth in front of the house. The boys watched awhile fascinated until the younger boy asked his brother what in the world was going on. The older boy smiled and said, "Oh, that's just Pa. *He said he'd mow the lawn come hell or high water!*"

14

## The Hickory Switch

Most old-time general stores have their resident characters and the store in Ruff Creek is no exception. Among the colorful bunch that frequent the place is Kissy Davin who, along with other distinctions, holds the coveted, unofficial title as Ruff Creek's top storyteller. Kissy possesses a fine imagination, a reliable sense of timing, and a consistently cheerful disposition. His unhurried style never fails to hold the listener's attention. Most importantly, he has a sure-fire instinct for what makes a good tale and doesn't always let the 'facts' get in the way of his creations. Some folks around Ruff Creek claim Kissy'd as soon climb a tree to tell a lie as stand on the ground to tell the truth. In short, Kissy is an artist.

One winter's day, a few of the boys were loafing down at the store. They were passing the time talking about one thing and another. After a bit, the conversation got onto the plight of modern education. Ansel started it off by saying that the trouble with education these days was that they'd gotten rid of the hickory switch.

"That's what I think!" Ansel went on. "Kids do whatever they want nowadays. Why, when I was in school, I felt the sting of that switch many a time. Makes me wince just thinking about it, but it sure did make you sit up and take notice."

With a collective nod of their sage heads, everyone agreed with Ansel's comments. Everyone, that is, but old Kissy. He just sat deep in thought and remained silent. As this was not his custom when such weighty subjects were being discussed, there was a great deal of curiosity expressed regarding his views.

15

"Well," said Kissy slowly and thoughtfully, "I just don't hold with what you fellows are saying."

"Well, why not?" asked Ansel.

"You see," continued Kissy, as if the thought pained him, "it's like this. I got hit only once with the hickory switch when I was in school, and it was for telling the truth!"

There was a moment of silence as these words were considered. Then Ansel replied, *"Well, Kissy, it sure did cure you!"*

## *Liver Medicine*

Over the years, the Ruff Creek General Store has sold just about everything folks have needed. When doctors were scarce in the country, the store stocked a wide variety of patent medicines. Some said these medicines worked wonders while others argued that they were next to useless. Back in the store's early days, they carried a line of medicine called "Dr. Pendleton's Liver Restorer". The advertisement for this miracle elixir, manufactured in Erie, Pennsylvania, claimed it would cure any ailment affecting the liver, that most delicate and important of organs, even those caused from the ravages of home made whiskey. As moonshine was readily available in Ruff Creek at the time, this medicine was always a good seller at the store, particularly with the coal miners.

One local miner, Buster Abcorn, took to using "Dr. Pendleton's Liver Restorer" and he'd tell anyone who'd listen that the medicine was a marvel and no mistake. He bought the stuff by the case, which contributed significantly to the store's revenues, and drank half a bottle a day religiously. He swore it cured him completely. But then tragedy struck. While working underground one day, the unfortunate Buster was crushed in a sudden roof fall. The poor man died instantly. It took several hours to dig him out and bring his lifeless body to the surface. *And then they had to cut him open and beat his liver to death with a stick! That's just how healthy it was after all that medicine!*

### *Hearing Aids*

Along with a variety of patent medicines, the general store experimented with a line of hearing aids for a time. A man named Abe was getting on in years and his hearing wasn't what it used to be. He came into the store one day and asked about purchasing one of the new-fangled hearing machines. Bob, who was minding the store that day, said they carried three different kinds. One was $100, another was $60, and one was $5.

"Well, what's the difference?" Abe wanted to know.

"The $100 hearing aid has twenty transistors and restores nearly 100% of your natural hearing, the $60 one has ten transistors and restores about 50% of your hearing," Bob replied.

Abe studied the two new hearing aids awhile, wondering which one would to buy.

"Well, what about the $5 one?" he then asked.

"Oh," said Bob, "that one's just a rubber plug with a string hanging from it. You stick the plug in your ear and stick the end of the string in your shirt pocket. *Makes folks TALK LOUDER!*"

17

## Fly In The Cider

Some years ago there was a farmer over in Deerlick who operated a small cider mill. Each autumn, when apples were easy to come by, he'd set to work, day and night, producing lots of fresh sweet cider which the Ruff Creek Store would sell to its customers by the gallon or glass.

One of the fellows who'd lived in Ruff Creek all his life and was a steady customer of the store was Ezzy Gabbert. He was a likable sort-of-fellow but was awful tight when it came to money, or anything else for that manner. Folks said he was so miserly "he'd skin a flea for the tallow". There was also a rumor that he'd make his kids take off their glasses when they weren't reading, so they wouldn't wear them out so fast.

One day Ezzy was down at the store with two of his buddies, Henry and Gil. It was late October, but the weather was unusually warm and they were sitting outside. They each had bought a cold, delicious glass of cider to drink. As they raised the glasses to their lips, each noticed a fly swimming around in his own glass. It nearly turned Henry's stomach. He got a spoon from inside the store and lifted the half-drowned insect out of the glass and pitched it away. He then drained the cider in a single long swallow. Gil didn't want to waste time going in for a spoon. He just took his finger and held the fly to the side of the glass while he drank his cider down. Ezzy looked quite put out. He reached into his drink and grabbed the cider-logged fly between his fingers. He held it up , slapping it on the back with his other hand, and said sternly, *"Spit it out!"*

## A Donation

On another occasion, the local minister from the Ruff Creek Church was out collecting money to purchase some frozen turkeys to give to needy families for Thanksgiving. He went into the general store to ask Ray for a donation and noticed Ezzy sitting in back by the meat counter.
"Morning, Ezzy," the minister said pleasantly. "Would you consider donating $5 to the Turkeys-for-Thanksgiving drive?"
Ezzy, who's as tight with money as bark on a tree, pretended his hearing was failing. "Sorry, Reverend, I didn't quite make out what you said."
The minister, however, wasn't going to be put off that easily and said much more loudly, "I said, Ezzy, would you donate $10 to the Turkeys-for-Thanksgiving drive?"
The old man replied in a mournful voice, *"I wish to Heaven I'd heard you the first time!"*

## Two Tramps

Two tramps came through Ruff Creek one summer. They were looking for a hand-out and happened on the Ezzy Gabbert place. Ezzy wasn't at home but his wife, Mabel, was. Now, if Ezzy was hard to get a dollar out of, Mabel was even worse. Ezzy said she was as tight as the backdoor on a Scottish bank.
One of the tramps said to his partner as they opened the front gate, "Bill, I've an idea. You get down on your hands and knees in the yard here and pretend

19

you're eating the grass, like a starving horse. They're bound to feel sorry for us and we'll get something good to eat."

Then the tramp went up and knocked on the door. Mabel opened the door and the man pointed to his friend and said, "Ma'am, we've been on the road a long time and we're desperate for something to eat. My friend there is so hungry, why he's eating the grass in your front yard."

The old woman replied without a pause, *"Mister, you can tell him the grass is a lot taller out back."*

## A Secret Ingredient

Harvey Deakins came into the store one day to buy some minnows and started bragging about how he'd come up with the best fishing idea that ever was. When Ray asked him about it, Harvey said, "It was more of an accident, than anything else. You see, I was out fishing on Ten Mile Creek yesterday. I was using the minnows I'd bought here and they were lively little fellows but I wasn't having a bit of luck. Ray, you know my wife, if I don't come home with some fresh fish after spending my day off on the river, (instead of doing them honey-do jobs she's always got ready, like 'honey, do this and honey, do that'), I'm in deep trouble. But them fish weren't biting. Hour after hour, I tried every trick I know without even a nibble. No luck at all."

"Well, what happened?" asked Ray, caught up in the tale by now.

"You know as well as anyone," went on Harvey, "I take a little drink now and again. Well I had some

20

first-rate moonshine with me on the river. I was sipping on the whiskey with my line in the water and it was growing dark. I was desperate when, all of a sudden, I had a brainstorm. If I enjoy the taste of moonshine, well, maybe a fish would take to it too. I took my last minnow and put him on the hook. Then I swished him around in the jar of whiskey and made my cast. I'm telling you the truth, Ray, that bait no sooner hit the water than something big grabbed it. The line zzzinged out and I had to hold onto my rod with both hands. What a fish, never felt such fight in my life. Pretty soon I tired the poor thing out and brought it up next to the boat. You may not believe it, Ray, but I had a ten-foot catfish on the end of my line! *And do you know that minnow had him by the throat and was choking him!"*

## Posey Reading the Newspaper

Back in the 1920's in Ruff Creek, there lived a man named Posey Wills. Posey had been born on a farm but had gone to work in the mines at an early age. He only went to school for a few years and wasn't able to read or write at all. This deficiency was a serious embarrassment to Posey throughout his life, even though it didn't affect how folks regarded him around Ruff Creek. Like many illiterate people, he'd try all kinds of subterfuges to hide the fact that he couldn't read. He even owned a pair of wire-rim glasses he'd found somewhere and he would put them on whenever something was given him to read. Of course, all the glasses did was make things blurry for the old man but it kept up appearances.

One day, Posey was down at the general store. He had his glasses on and was holding a newspaper up in front of him, pretending to read it. This was the heyday of the fancy ocean-going luxury liners and there was a picture on the front page of a new ship that had been launched that week in New York. Another miner named Sim came in the store. He'd just come off his shift in the mine and his face was still black with coal dust. He looked over at Posey and noticed that the old man was holding the newspaper upside down and didn't know it. It was too good an opportunity to pass up and he decided to have some fun with the old-timer.

Sim said in a casual way, so everyone in the store could hear, "Howdy, Posey, what's in the news today?" The old man replied, *"Well, I can tell you one thing. There's certainly  been a terrible shipwreck!"*

### Refusing A Job

Ray worked  for his dad  down at the Ruff  Creek Store when he was a youngster. Now that he runs the store himself, he always tries to help the young people of the area by providing employment whenever possible. A few years back a teenager named Billy Meighen approached Ray for a job. He was a healthy, good-sized boy but Ray had all the help he needed just then. Day after day the young fellow would stop by the store and ask about a job.

Finally another boy who had been working at the store for several years graduated from high school. He decided to join the Air Force and told Ray he'd be leaving soon. Ray decided to offer his job to Billy.

The next day when Billy came into the store, Ray told him the good news.

"I guess I can finally put you to work if you're still of a mind," said Ray.

"What kind of work do you want me to do?" the boy asked.

"To start with," went on Ray, "you can help pump gas and watch the cash register when I'm in the back. Other times, you can stock shelves and sweep the floor."

"How much are you going to pay me for all this work?" the young man wanted to know.

"Well now," answered Ray thoughtfully, "reckon I'll pay you whatever you're worth."

Oh, that won't do," replied Billy. *"I don't work for that kind of money."*

## Death Rate

A man from the city stopped at the general store one afternoon to buy some gasoline. As he was paying for his purchase, he remarked, "This sure is lovely country you've got around here. Everything's so green and the air smells wonderful! Bet folks here take life easy and enjoy themselves."

Ray's wife, Karen, was minding the store at the time and agreed it was a nice place to live. At this, the man went on about the city.

"Seems people in town are always racing around and worried all the time. It's got to be healthier to live in the country. What's the death-rate in these parts, anyhow?" he asked.

Karen replied, "Oh, I reckon it's the same here as anywhere else. *About one to a person."*

23

## Thirty Miles to Town

Another city fellow was driving through the country one time and stopped at a store on the other side of Cannonsburg to ask directions to a certain town. The storeowner told him it was thirty miles straight down the road. The fellow drove on and on but never came to the town. After more than an hour, he stopped at the Ruff Creek General Store and asked Ray, the owner, how to get to the town he was looking for.

"Well, mister," said Ray, "that town's about thirty miles straight down the road."

At this, the city fellow got hotter than a hen eating chilli peppers. "Why, I stopped at a store up the road more than an hour ago and he told me it was thirty miles to that town. Now, you're telling me the same thing!"

Ray calmly answered, *"Leastwise, mister, you can see we ain't lying!"*

## Peanuts in the Bowl

When Jack Stockdale retired from running the Ruff Creek General Store, his son, Ray, took it over. Still, the old man would often help out minding the store when his son had to go someplace on business. On one such occasion, a lady came into the store saying that her car had broken down a mile or so up the road. Mr. Stockdale couldn't leave the woman without help, so he put a note on the door saying he'd be back soon, and went to see what was wrong with the car. He closed up the cash register but didn't lock the door. He

24

figured if anyone wanted to buy something, they'd wait for him to return or just leave the money on the counter.

Soon after he left, a young fellow named Calvin came into the store. He needed to buy some chain to hang up a porch swing he'd just made as a birthday present for his mother. There were several big spools of different size chain in the back of the store but, with nobody around to help him, Calvin couldn't locate the cutters. As there wasn't anything more he could do until he got some chain, he decided to wait.

It was well past noon and Calvin had been working so hard getting the swing built that he'd gone without his dinner. He was awfully hungry and his stomach was growling like an old tractor with a bad muffler. He then noticed there was a bowl of peanuts on the counter. They were the shelled variety and look mighty inviting to the boy. He took one and ate it. It tasted pretty good. Like most folks, Calvin kept right on eating the peanuts, one after another, until they were all gone. He suspected that the peanuts belonged to the old man and he started to feel guilty. When Mr. Stockdale finally returned, Calvin confessed his crime and offered to make restitution.

"I reckon that bowl of peanuts belonged to you, Mr. Stockdale," said the young man. "I only meant to eat a couple but, before I knew what I was doing, I'd finished the lot. I'll be glad to buy you some more."

"Oh, that's alright," replied the old man good-naturedly. "Why, since I've lost my teeth, I can't eat them things anyhow. Now I only buy them candy-coated peanuts. Then I suck the coverings off and *spit what's left into the bowl.*"

25

# CHAPTER TWO

# Country Wit and Wisdom

City-slicker: *Say, old man, does this road go to Little Rock?*
Farmer: *That road's never gone nowhere.*
City-slicker: *Well, have you lived here all your life?*
Farmer: *Not yet.*
City-slicker: *You sure don't know a whole heck of alot, do you?*
Farmer: *No, but I ain't lost!*

  - old medicine show skit, the Arkansas Traveler

## *Whole Blind*

Some years ago, two brothers from Greene County went up to Pittsburgh to find work. A new steel mill was doing some hiring but, when the brothers arrived, they found about six hundred men lined up to apply. Finally the older brother, Judd, was called in to talk with the personnel director.

The man looked him over and asked, "Do you drink?"
"Never have," Judd answered.
"Do you show up on time?"
"Always have."
"Ever done this kind of work before?"
"No, but I learn quick. Just need to have it explained once." "Alright," the director said, "I'll give you a job if you can answer two questions. Now if I poked out one of your eyes, what would you be?"
"Half blind," Judd answered.
"That's right," the man said. "And if I poked out both your eyes, what would you be?"
"Whole blind," the older brother replied.
"That's also correct," said the director, making some notes on a pad in front of him. "You've got a job, mister. Go over to payroll and sign up. While you're at it, please tell the next fellow to come in."
Now the man didn't know the next fellow was Judd's brother, Edwin. So Judd said to his brother, "Now look here, Edwin, it's easy. There are two questions and the answers are, 'half blind' and 'whole blind'. You give them answers and we'll both have jobs!"
Edwin went into the office and the man asked him whether he drank, showed up on time, and so on. He said he'd give him a job if he could answer two

questions.

"If I cut off one of your ears, what would you be?"

"Half blind," Edwin shot back.

The man looked up from his paperwork surprised and said, "That's not right. Where are you from anyhow?"

"Greene County," replied the young man with pride.

"Well," said the director thoughtfully, "that's a long way to come for a job of work. I don't usually give a second chance but, if you can answer the next question correctly, you'll get the job anyway. Now, think about it. If I cut off both your ears, what would you be?"

Edwin looked him in the eye and said, "Whole blind."

The director shook his head slowly and said, " I'm sorry fella, but that's not right. I can't hire you. But before you leave, you've just got to tell me how you figure you'd be whole blind if I cut off both your ears?"

"Well, it's easy," Edwin answered. *"My hat'd fall down over my eyes!"*

Well, they gave him the job of foreman and he recently took over as president of that company!

### The Antique Dealer and the Cat

There was  an antique dealer from Sewickley one time who drove down to Greene County to take in an auction. She knew everything there was to know about antique glass and she purchased a few pieces to resell later in the city. On her way home she stopped at the general store to get some gas and noticed a poster on the bulletin board about a garage sale nearby.  She hunted up the house but there wasn't much to look at; an old bike with a flat tire, a black-and-white television set with a missing knob, and some other used items of

29

questionable value. But just as she was about to leave, she noticed an ornate, red glass bowl sitting on the floor in the corner of the garage. A small yellow and white cat was lapping milk out of it. Even at a distance, the dealer knew the bowl was quite rare and very valuable. She didn't want to let on, however, that she was interested in it for she knew the price would go up.

"Why, bless my stars," she said to the woman doing the selling, "what a pretty little cat that is! Why, it's exactly like the cat I used to have when I was a little girl. You couldn't tell them apart. Would you consider selling that cat to me? I would love for my little girl to have a cat just like the one I had when I was her age. I'll give you $10 for it."

The woman said she wasn't sure she wanted to sell the animal. They had lots of cats around the place but she thought it might be her son's favorite.

"I know it's not worth it," replied the antique dealer, " but I'll give you $20 for it. It's for sentimental reasons."

The woman finally agreed and the antique dealer picked up the cat and carried over to her car. She came back with her purse and took out a $20 bill which she handed to the woman.

Then, with her purse still open, she said, as an afterthought, "While we're at it, let me give you a dollar for that glass bowl over there."

"No, I'm sorry," said the other woman, "but that bowl's not for sale."

The city woman persisted. "I know it's just an ordinary glass bowl but it's something the little cat is familiar with. It'll help it adjust to its new home. I'll tell you what, I'll give you $5 for it."

"No," said the woman, "it's not for sale at any price." Realizing the woman's mind was set and she wasn't about to give in, the dealer lost her temper. Here she had a cat that she didn't want which had cost her $20. The truth was, she didn't even have a daughter and didn't like cats in the first place. Exasperated, she said, "And why in the world won't you sell me that bowl?" "Well, you see," said the other woman thoughtfully, *"if I sold you that bowl, I couldn't sell any more cats."*

### Tellin' Time

Another time a couple from Pittsburgh drove down to Greene County to take in a horse show in Waynesburg. They decided to take Route 19 back home, instead of the interstate, so they could enjoy the countryside a little. But just before reaching Ruff Creek, their car ran out of gas. It was a beautiful summer evening and neither of them were very worried about it. They started walking and soon passed a farm where they saw an old woman milking a Jersey cow. The animal was tied to the fence and the woman was sitting on a three-legged stool squirting milk into a bucket.
"Excuse me," the man called over to her, "but could you please tell us the time?"
The woman nodded and bent down low under the cow. She pushed up one of the cow's teats, and then the other one, and squinted.
"Just six o'clock, " she answered. The couple just stood staring.
"How in the world did she know the time by that cow's udder?" the wife wanted to know.
"I have no idea," said her husband, "let's go ask her."

31

They walked over to where the farm-woman was milking and inquired about how she knew the time by the cow's udder. "Well," the woman said, looking a bit puzzled, "I can't tell you as easy as I can show you. Have you ever milked a cow before?" she asked the city woman.

"No," was the lady's nervous reply.

"Well, there's nothing to it," continued the old woman, getting up and giving her the stool. "That's right, just take hold and don't be scared. Old Muley won't kick you."

The wife did as she was told.

"O.K. now, bend way down. Push up one quarter, that's right, push up the other. Now, squint. *Do you see that clock on the barn wall over there?*"

### Artie's Haircut

There's a barber in Ruff Creek named Don Lemly and his barbershop is in a small, one-room building just up from the store. One Saturday morning a young fellow named Artie Honkle came in to get his hair cut. Several other men were there before him and Artie had to wait. He got to reading in one of the magazines about some "punk rock" band and this gave him an idea. He was forever poking fun at people.

When his turn came, Artie got up in the barber's chair and Lemly asked him what kind of haircut he wanted.

"I'll tell you what, Don," he answered, in a voice loud enough for everyone to hear, "I want you to cut my hair real short on the right side, like they do it in the Marines, with short, little stubbly things sticking out, but leave it long on the other side, hanging down over my ear. Then I want three long pointy things in back going down under my collar. Then finish it off with a bald spot on top, about the size of a silver dollar."

The barber looked distressed and said, "Artie, I don't think I can cut your hair that way."

Then Artie replied, "Why, that's funny, Don. *You cut it that way last month!*"

## Meeting Up With A Bear

One time Artie and his older brother, Jay, went up to Bedford County to do some fishing. It's wild and mountainous country up there and the bears are as thick as blackberries. As they were walking through some woods on their way to a remote spot on the river, the boys suddenly heard a crashing sound and a big, old she-bear came charging out of a thicket straight at them. She looked meaner than a one-eyed drunk on Saturday night and ready to kill.

The boys froze, Artie in front of Jay, and the bear came to a stop just a few feet from them, eyeing them both like a big tomcat watching a mouse. The brothers figured that they must have unknowingly come near the bear's cubs somehow, that would explain her being so out-of-sorts. They also knew, that if they made any sudden move, she'd be all over them.

Then from behind, Jay could see Artie reach up carefully into his backpack and take out a white tennis shoe. Very slowly, watching the growling bear every second, the younger boy managed to pull off one of his boots and slip on the shoe. Then he reached again into his pack and brought out another tennis shoe. Still careful not to alarm the bear, Artie removed his other boot and put on the shoe.  By this time Jay couldn't stand it any longer.

"What, in heaven's name, do you think you're do-ing?" said Jay in a hoarse whisper.  "You know you can't outrun that bear even in tennis shoes!"

"I know," answered his younger brother over his shoulder, without turning his head.  *"I don't have to outrun the bear.  I've just got to outrun you!"*

## A Pig of Unusual Size

O scar is an accomplished trader from Ruff  Creek who has for many years traveled about the county searching out bargains.  He'll trade for just about anything, from a dozen eggs to a team of horses, a barn full of hay, a Remington pocket knife, or an old fiddle, whatever he can make a little something on.

He's also willing to play the fool as well as the next man and is always trying to outsmart another Green County trader named Charlie.

Several years ago the two traders were over at the stock auction in Waynesburg.  They were sitting together up in the gallery when a huge red hog was brought in. As the auctioneer started the bidding, Charlie remarked that it was the biggest hog he'd ever seen.

"Why,"replied Oscar, "I've got a pig that you can't even touch his back when your standing on a chair!"

Charlie said he wouldn't call Oscar a liar but he found such a thing hard to believe.

"Believe it or not, it's true." said the trader with con-viction.  Charlie stated that if Oscar had such a pig, he would swap any two of his own hogs for it.  Oscar agreed to the deal and they shook hands on it.

Later that evening they went over to Oscar's place. The men went into the house and fetched a chair and carried it out to the barn.

"Now get up on that chair," said Oscar, "while I go and get that pig." Charlie stood up on the chair and waited. He felt a little stupid standing there on the chair alone in the barn but he was determined to see this unusual pig.

Pretty soon Oscar returned carrying the smallest runt of a pig that ever was. He placed it on the floor and said with considerable satisfaction, "There you go Charlie, *now I bet you can't touch that pig's back while standing on that chair!*"

## A Profitable Raffle

Another time Oscar had an opportunity to purchase an old farm for $1,500. Farmland was easy to buy for many years around Greene County for it seemed everyone wanted to live in town. Oscar wanted the place a great deal but couldn't lay his hands on the cash money to buy it. He owned an old workhorse named Ted that was a dandy. Ted could work up in the woods skidding heavy logs or pull a cultivator through a field of corn without trampling a single cornstalk. He'd respond to voice commands, like "gee" for right and "haw" for left, and Oscar could drop the traces and let the horse go on by himself with complete confidence. Everyone around Ruff Creek knew what a fine animal he was but wouldn't give Oscar $1,500 for him.

One day Oscar had an inspiration! He'd been noticing how some of the churches made good money from the different raffles they put on and he decided to take a shot at one himself. He went to the printer in Waynesburg and had a number of tickets made up. Then in early October, he put several big sign up around Ruff Creek which read:

---

**BUY A CHANCE TO WIN TED THE HORSE!**

**$2.00 A CHANCE**

**DRAWING TO BE HELD AT THE**

**RUFF CREEK GENERAL STORE**

**NOVEMBER 15th**

---

The idea turned out to be a great success. Tickets went faster than maple syrup at a Kiwanis Pancake Supper. The only problem was, Ted proved somewhat contrary. A week before the official drawing, the poor animal took a case of the heaves and died.

Then Charlie, who'd been away in Ohio visiting relatives at the time, returned. He was down at the Ruff Creek Store and, seeing Oscar there, he thought he'd needle him some about his big scheme.

"How'd your raffle go, Oscar?" he asked pleasantly.

"Oh, quite well," the trader replied, with a smile of satisfaction. "I made enough money from that one deal to buy the farm and another workhorse, besides!"

Charlie was somewhat confused. "Why, didn't that old animal up and died on you before the drawing?"

"Yes it did, the poor thing," said Oscar, "but I'm no quitter. I just continued selling chances all the same."

"Well, weren't folks angry when they found out about the horse being dead?" asked Charlie in disbelief.

"Oh no," answered Oscar, "just the fellow that won him - *and I gave him his money back.*"

36

## The Lost Wallet

One time Oscar was at a big farm auction in Holbrook. He went over to the table where they served the food and ordered a piece of cherry pie. When he went to pay for it, however, he was alarmed to find that he'd lost his wallet. He spent an anxious hour scouting around the yard by the house and out in the barn but without any luck.

Greene County is a small farm community and everyone pretty much knows everyone else. So Oscar asked the auctioneer to make an announcement.

"Ladies and gentlemen, listen up," the auctioneer said over the P.A. system. "A man here has lost his wallet. He says there was over $800 in cash in it, along with his credit cards and driver's license. He says he'll give $50 to whoever finds it."

There was a moment's silence when someone else shouted, *"I'll give $75!"*

## The New Minister

A young minister graduated with top honors from the Theological Seminary in Pittsburgh and was sent down to Ruff Creek to preach. On his first Sunday he went over early to the red brick church and waited for the congregation to turn up. The minutes ticked by but, when 11:00 arrived, the time for the worship service to begin, only one man was sitting out in the pews. The young minister waited awhile longer but no one else showed up.

Finally, in frustration, he said to the man, "If I was a

member of this church, I'd be down-right embarrassed. Here I've come all this way to preach to you people and you're the only one with the courtesy to show up. What do you think I should do?"

"Well, Reverend," the man replied, in a slow, thoughtful way. "I'm nothing but an old farmer. But when I go out to feed my cattle, I feed 'em."

The young man was somewhat sobered by this and said, "Alright, my friend, take out your hymnal, we'll have us a service."

They started out singing "Amazing Grace", just the two of them, without an organ or anything. The minister continued on through the order of worship and then gave his first sermon with zeal and conviction.

An hour later, when he'd finished, the minister asked the old man what he thought of the service.

"Well, Reverend, I'm nothing but an old farmer." the man said again in his unhurried voice. "When I go out to feed my cattle, I feed 'em. But if only one shows up, I don't give him the whole load!"

### Insurance Money

One summer Bud Hickman from Prosperity was sitting on the beach in Ocean City, New Jersey, relaxing and soaking up some sun. His wife had gone to get a couple of hot dogs and cokes and the kids were playing in the water. There was a fellow sitting nearby and pretty soon they'd started up a conversation. As it turned out, the other fellow was from western Pennsylvania too.

"What brings you down here?" Bud asked.

"Well, to tell you the truth," the man said, "my house

caught fire last month and I just received a $20,000 check from the insurance company. My wife and I have never been to the beach, so we just took a little of the money and treated ourselves to a vacation."

"Now that is a coincidence!" said Bud. "We lost our house in a flood this spring and we received $40,000 from our insurance company. That's where we got the money to come down here ourselves!"

The other man appeared thoughtful awhile and then asked, *"Tell me, how do you start a flood?"*

## A Good Friend

Anyone who has ever lived or worked with a dog for very long knows what a strong bond can develop between a human and his four-legged friend. There was an old bachelor some years ago living up on Crayne's Run who had a dog named Buck. The dog helped with the chores around the farm, such as driving the cows in for the evening milking, and served as a faithful companion for the old man for many years. Finally old age caught up with Buck and he passed away.

The next day the old man drove over to the Baptist minister's house. He knocked on the door and asked in a respectful way when the preacher answered, "Reverend, my old dog died last night and I've got him in the back of my pickup truck. I was hoping that you could say some words over him when I go to bury him."

"Oh no," said the preacher aghast, "I couldn't hardly do that! It just wouldn't be right to read Holy Scripture for a dead animal."

The old man took the answer without a complaint but

then asked if the preacher could direct him to the Methodist minister's house.

"What do you want to know that for?" queried the Baptist.

"Well, you see," went on the farmer, "I've saved up $50 cash money to pay some preacher to say words over Buck's grave and I mean to see it done."

"Hold on," said the preacher excitedly. *"You didn't tell me your dog was a Baptist!"*

## *Fishing In a Dry Field*

A doctor from Pittsburgh was driving through Greene County one time looking to purchase some property for a summer home. It was a beautiful day as he drove out along Rte. 221 from Ruff Creek, taking in the countryside. Just before reaching Dunn's Station, however, he happened to notice a fellow up from the road fishing in a dry field. His curiosity aroused, the doctor pulled over and watched.

The fisherman seemed completely absorbed in what he was doing, contentedly casting away with his rod and reel. It didn't seem to be some sort of practice. There was live bait dangling from his hook. But there wasn't a drop of water to be seen anywhere.

The doctor finally decided the fellow needed help and drove on down to the next house. He blew his horn and a farmer came out and asked what he wanted.

"There's a man up the road a ways who's fishing in a dry field. Do you know who he is?"

"Why, I sure do," said the farmer. "That's my crazy brother. *Reckon I'll just have to get in the boat and go get him!"*

## A Smart Judge

Back during the Depression there was a judge named A. R. Phillips who presided over the court in Waynesburg. Unlike many other judges during those difficult times, Judge Phillips often displayed a sympathetic understanding for the plight of the common man. One particular case bore this out.

A fellow by the name of Oak Jeffries worked in Waynesburg as a maintenance man for the school board. He supported a large family on his meager salary and would often have only a piece of bread and a cold boiled potato for his mid-day meal. He devised a clever plan, however, to help make this simple repast seem more substantial.

At noon each day he would go downtown and sit by the back door of the Fort Jackson Hotel to eat his meal. The Fort Jackson served the wealthier people in town, coal operators, lawyers, and the like. The rich, varied aromas of fine foods being prepared would waft out to Oak as he sat on the curb. Since the sense of smell adds a great deal to the enjoyment of food to start with, Oak's plain fare would take on the aspects of a feast.

Everything would have been fine had it not been for the restaurant's manager. He was a prissy sort-of-fellow and it irked him no end that Jeffries was enjoying himself this way at his expense. He ordered Jeffries to leave on several occasions but Oak refused, saying it was a public street and he had every right to be there. Finally in a rage of frustration, the manager went up to the police station and demanded that Oak be arrested. An officer followed him back to the hotel and, when Oak refused to move, he took him into custody.

41

The next day the case was brought before Judge Phillips. He first asked the manager what charge he was bringing against Jeffries.

"Theft, your honor," the manager said firmly. "This man sits behind my restaurant each day and enjoys the smells of my kitchen with his food. Now I buy only the finest ingredients and pay my cooks top-dollar to prepare the delicious meals we serve. This man has never paid a cent for the pleasure he gets from my investment and work, it's just plain robbery!"

The judge then spoke to Jeffries. "Is there any truth in what this man is saying?" Judge Phillips inquired.

"Your Honor," said Oak, "I've never stolen anything in my life. I just didn't see any harm in it, is all."

The judge then recessed the court for half an hour to consider the case.

When court came back into session, Judge Phillips asked both the plaintiff and the defendant to approach the bench.

"I am most disturbed by what I have heard here today," he began, with great seriousness. "Mr. Jeffries, do you have any money on you at this time?"

Oak reached into his pocket and took out several small coins which he handed to the judge.

"Thank you," said the judge. He then he addressed the restaurant manager, "Now, sir, if you would stand a little closer." The manager obeyed. Then the judge took the coins, cupped in his hand, and shook them next to the man's ear.

"Can you hear that?" asked the judge. "Now sir, you have been paid in full, the sound of his money for the smell of your food."

Judge Phillips then returned the coins to Oak and said, *"Case dismissed."*

## The Opinionated Juror

In most rural communities, such as Greene County, folks tend to know each other quite well. One time, several years ago, a case was brought before the court involving two local coal speculators. One had accused the other of fraud in relation to some coal properties he had recently purchased. It seemed someone had doctored the survey papers leaving the unhappy and furious buyer with a great deal less coal under the ground then he'd thought he'd acquired. The case was to go before a jury and Judge A. R. Phillips was presiding.

During jury selection, the lawyer for the plaintiff was questioning a prospective juror from Kuhntown.

"Mr. Whitting, do you happen to know the defendant in this case?"

"I sure do," was the man's quick reply. "He's the biggest cheat and liar in this county, and that's a fact! Why, I'd as soon believe a politician's promise as that scoundrel!"

Some laughter broke out in the court room and Judge Phillips had to bang his gavel to quiet it. Then the lawyer for the defense rose and addressed the same man.

"Well, sir, are you by any chance acquainted with the plaintiff in this case?"

"Yes, sir, I am," the man answered. "He's the worst rascal and drunk in these parts. I wouldn't trust that no-good if my life depended on it. I swear he'd sell his own mother and charge extra for the shipping!"

At this Judge Phillips called the two lawyers up to the bench and said, "If either of you ask Mr. Whitting what he thinks of me, *I'll cite you for contempt!*"

43

## Poisoned Watermelons

One of the crops Ezzy Gabbert is the most proud of is his watermelons. He has a big field set aside for them down by the main road and he tends to their cultivation with patient and loving care. The delectable fruit, however, has proved to be too great a temptation for some of the younger citizens of Ruff Creek to withstand. Each year, when the melons are at their sweetest and ready to pick, the kids slip over the fence in the dead of night and make off with a few. It doesn't amount to much in terms of the overall harvest but it makes Ezzy hot enough to boil water.

One year, however, Ezzy had a novel idea. He went to the store and bought some paint. He then made up a sign that read:

---

**Warning!**
**In this field is one poisoned watermelon!**
**- signed Ezra Gabbert**

---

He nailed the sign to a fence post where all could see. The next morning he went down to the field to see if any of his melons were missing. They were all there, every last one. But then he noticed that someone had tampered with his sign. It now said,

---

**Warning!**
**In this field is one poisoned watermelon!**
**- signed Ezra Gabbert**
**P.S.**
**Now, there are two!**

---

## The Lost Preacher

A preacher from over in Ohio stopped in at the Ruff Creek General Store one day to ask directions. Ray was back in the storeroom stacking up some horse feed while several of the local fellows were passing the time sitting on the gossip bench playing cards.

"Excuse me," said the preacher politely, "could you please tell me how to get to the nearest post office?"

One of the men answered, "You're almost there. Just go down that road to the right a ways and you'll see it." The preacher thanked him and then noticed with dismay that there was some money on the bench next to the men. He realized they were betting on the card game.

"I'm a minister," he said, "and I'd like to ask you something. How do you expect to get to heaven if you play cards like that and gamble?"

The same fellow who had given the directions responded, "Well, preacher, *how do you expect to get to heaven if you can't even find the Post Office?*"

## Giving a Farmer a Ride

One cold and snowy winter day a farmer named Tom Holland was walking along the road on his way to the general store. There were steep snow banks on both sides of the road left by the plows and it was hard to get over for traffic. A young fellow who was late for work came flying along in his car. He was going much too fast for the dangerous conditions and, just as he reached the old man, he hit a patch of ice. The car

45

lurched and he caught the farmer's pant leg on the bumper of his car. He dragged Tom down the road a good distance, skidding along on the packed snow. Finally the car came to a stop. The frightened young man jumped out and helped the farmer back onto his feet.

"Mister, I swear I never meant to do that," he said. "I just couldn't help sliding into you. I sure hope you ain't hurt or nothing?"

Brushing the snow and gravel from his clothes, Tom said that, besides being scraped up and a little bruised, he was alright. He felt his arms and legs and said there didn't seem to be anything broken. The relieved young man apologized over and over again and asked if there was someplace he could take the old man.

"No, that's not necessary," said the farmer, *"I reckon I've ridden with you far enough!"*

## *The Doctor's Diagnosis*

There was an old fellow named Levi Hall who lived off Rte. 221 on the way over to Dunn's Station. He was up in years and had lived by himself all his life. He made a profession of being difficult to get along with. Most of his neighbors had gotten used to it and didn't give it another moment's thought.

One day Levi called for the doctor to come over to the house. When Doc Pierce arrived, he found the old man lying in bed under heaps of covers.

The doctor put his bag down and approached the patient. He then said in his best bedside manner, "Morning Levi, and what seems to be the matter with you?"

46

"Well, seeing as you're the doctor," replied the old man, "you tell me!"

Doc Pierce thought about this for a few seconds and then said, "Well, Levi, you wouldn't happen to have Doctor MacPherson's telephone number around here someplace, would you?"

"What you want his number for?" said Levi irritably. "He's not a people doctor, he's a veterinarian."

"Yes, I know that, Levi," answered the doctor, *"but he's the only one can tell what's wrong with a jackass just by looking at him."*

## A Quick Answer

Back in horse and buggy days there was a blacksmith named Grover Hardy who lived over in Lippincott. One day he was working in his forge making some horseshoes for a pair of Belgians a local farmer owned. He pulled a large red-hot shoe from the coal fire with his tongs and laid it up on the windowsill to cool while he went to work on another.

A young boy nicknamed, "Thumper", happened to come along and saw the new horseshoe. He was a curious type of lad and so he reached up and grabbed it. With the hot metal burning his fingers, the boy gave a yell of surprise and flung it far away from him. The blacksmith, who had seen what had happened, decided to tease the boy.

In a slow, measured way, he said with a grin, "Kind of hot, ain't it, son?"

"No," said Thumper calmly, *"it just don't take long to look at a horseshoe."*

## The Texan and the Farmer

Hobart Davies was working out in his garden one day digging potatoes. It was good harvest for the clay soil of Greene County and he had several mounds of new potatoes next to him. He was taking a short break to catch his wind and have a drink of water when a heavyset fellow came walking up.

"Afternoon, Mr. Davies," said the stranger agreeably, "I'm with the National Equity Insurance Company. I stopped up at the house and your pretty wife said I'd find you out here."

Hobart had little use for salesman of any kind and there was something about the man's manner and accent that put him off.

"Where'd you from anyway, mister?" Hobart wanted to know.

"Why, I live in Pittsburgh now but I was raised up in the great state of Texas!" said the salesman with pride. Hobart said he'd never been to Texas but he'd heard about it.

Thus encouraged, the man began to talk at length about the Lone Star State, expounding upon its many virtues and achievements. After working himself up to a fevered pitch, the insurance salesman said, "Why, Mr. Davies, just compare your itty-bitty potatoes here to the ones we grow down home. Why Texas potatoes are as big as cantaloupes!"

Hobart thought about this a few seconds and then said with certainty, *"Reckon you grow 'em just like us. Big enough to fit your mouth."*

Needless to say, the salesman didn't do any business in Ruff Creek that day.

48

## Vernon's Conscience

Vernon Strunk works for a large coal company that operates a mine near Ruff Creek. As purchasing agent for the company, he often deals with a certain salesman for a mine equipment outfit out of Pittsburgh. One day, after placing a substantial order, the salesman presented Vernon with a beautiful quartz wristwatch as a token of his firm's appreciation. Vernon looked at the watch longingly for awhile but then handed it back.

"John, I appreciate the gesture," he said, "but I can't accept this watch in good conscience."

"Well, why not, Vernon?" asked the concerned salesman.

Vernon explained, "You see, John, it just wouldn't look right for me to accept such a valuable gift when I work for the company that gives you folks so much business. No, I just can't take it, thanks all the same."

The salesman thought about it for a few minutes and then said with a sly grin, "Well, since I can't give it to you, Vernon, why don't I just sell it to you? No one one could complain about that, could they? I'll just sell you this watch for a dollar. How's that sound?"

Vernon considered the offer and then replied, *"Well, in that case, I'll take two."*

## Taking Out A Loan

Old man Wagner made a bundle of money when a big coal company bought up some of his farm for a railroad right-of-way. Folks said the cagey farmer took them to the cleaners by the time the papers were signed. He then sold off his stock and farm equipment and started taking life easy.

One time he went to see the sights in New York City. He went into the main office of the Chase Manhattan Bank while he was there and asked to see the loan manager.

"I want to take out a $1,000 loan," stated the old farmer when asked what he wanted.

"Do you happen to have an account with us," inquired the banker.

Wagner said he'd never been to New York before.

"Well, do you have any collateral we might use to secure the loan?" asked the banker.

The farmer then placed an automobile title on the man's desk along with a set of car keys. "We don't need to waste time filling out a bunch of paperwork. Outside is a brand-new Lincoln Continental. You hold the car until I pay you back. Agreed?"

The surprised banker said it was highly unusual but finally approved the loan. Wagner left with his check. Later that day, the banker ran a credit check and found out the farmer was a millionaire!

A week later Wagner returned and said he wished to pay off the loan. The banker calculated the interest and it came to $17.50. The old man wrote out a check for the whole amount and asked for his car keys back. But as he was about to leave, the banker addressed him. "It's none of my business," he said, " but I did some checking up on you. You're a rich man. Why did you need to borrow $1,000 from us?"

"Oh, that's easy, " answered the old man, *"where else could I park a Lincoln Continental in downtown Manhattan for $17.50 a week!"*

## A Quiet Lesson

When Lester's wife passed away, the old man stopped coming to church on Sunday mornings. He'd always attended the worship service before then and the young minister was concerned. He waited several weeks and, when Lester still failed to show, he decided to pay the old man a visit. One of the deacons of the church that had known the old man for years warned the preacher that Lester was one of the quietest men he'd ever met.

"Why, old Lester just don't waste words is all. And he don't appreciate others who do."

The next day the minister went up to Lester's house late in the afternoon. It was a cold, blustery day and the farmer was inside staying warm by the fire. He answered the door without saying a word and motioned for the minister to follow him back into the house. Lester dragged a chair over for the young man to sit on and he sat down in another. Neither man said a word, they just stared into the fire.

After awhile the minister leaned forward and took hold of the poker. Sticking it into the fire and hooking a glowing coal, he carefully pulled it out onto the hearthstone. Slowly, the red hot coal began to cool. It soon had turned a dull lifeless grey. Nothing was said. The young minister then took the poker and pushed the coal back into the fire. In just a moment, it began glowing a bright red color again. The minister replaced the poker and put on his hat and coat. He left without saying a word.

The next Sunday Lester showed up for church.

51

# CHAPTER THREE

# The Taller the Better

*Old folks, old folks, better go to bed,*
*Don't put ideas in the young folks'heads.*

- old fiddle tune, Soldier's Joy

## The Beautiful Dollhouse

Mrs. Louise Davis runs a small antique business up the road from the general store. She'd often say that antiques aren't all they're cracked up to be but as city folks seemed to want them, and pay good money to boot, she'll oblige them. She keeps her collection of old rocking chairs, corner cupboards, mantle clocks, and depression glass in a large barn down next to the road.

One Saturday a man from Ohio stopped by to look over her goods. He wound up purchasing a few small items. Then, as he was about to leave, he mentioned that he collected dollhouses and wondered if she had any. Louise said she had one that had been hers as a child.

"It's one of the finest I've ever seen, even if I do say so myself," she said.

The man said he'd very much like to see it, if it wasn't too much trouble.

"I'd be happy to show it to you," Louise said, "but it's not for sale, you understand."

They went into the house and climbed up some narrow stairs into the attic. Louise removed a white sheet revealing the beautiful large dollhouse. It was exquisitely made! It stood about three feet high and was the most realistic-looking miniature house the man had ever seen. He wondered who had built such an amazing dollhouse.

"That was my father's doing," Louise said. "You see, back in 1925 he built it for our family to live in." As the man seemed confused, she continued. "It all started one summer when Pa was cutting hay. He was using a team of horses and a McCormick mowing machine. He'd broken something on the mower and was leaning over working on it when he noticed the smell of cucumbers. He had grown up on a farm and knew what that particular smell meant. Turning slowly around, he saw an enormous copperhead snake coming straight at him. He had no idea if a snake could get rabies, but this one sure acted mad. It was nearly on top of him when he gave a jump. The snake struck at him but missed and, instead, sank its long fangs into the wooden tongue of the mowing machine. Pa took a stick and killed it and threw its body over the hill. But by the time he returned to hitch up the team, the wooden tongue had nearly doubled in size. The potent deadly poison from the virulent snake had caused the wood to swell. It went on like that most of the afternoon until the tongue was as fat around as a saw log!"

"My father eventually took it down to the sawmill, run by the Mitchell boys and had them saw it up into different size boards,"Louise continued. "Unbelievable as it sounds, my father got enough wood from that one log to build a new house, it was that big! He paid some carpenters to help him and he managed to complete the house by fall."

"Then," added Louise in a wistful voice, "he decided to paint the house before we moved in. Ma always wanted a red house, you understand. But my father never reckoned on the turpentine in the paint. Sure enough, it drew all the swelling out of that wood caused by the snake poison and the house shrunk down to the size it is now. All he could do was give it to me for a dollhouse to play with. It was several years again before he could afford to build a proper house for our family."

## A Good Shot

Monty Wallace was born and raised in Greene County. He saw the first electric light, first automobile, and first telephone come into the country. Since childhood he had spent many hours up in the woods hunting game of all kinds. His skill with a rifle or shotgun was legendary. He won every turkey shoot and other shooting contest in western Pennsylvania for years on end.

His favorite rifle was an old muzzle-loader he'd inherited from his father. It had been made by a Dutchman near Lancaster and had been in his family since the late 1700's. It was hand-rifled and shot truer than a preacher's sermon. When modern repeating rifles first came on the market, Monty wouldn't have a thing to do with them. Possessing as sharp an eye and steady a hand as he did, he figured he never needed more than one shot to take his quarry.

Sometime in the 1920's Monty and his hunting buddy, Woody Mayl, were doing some hunting. They liked to stay out several days at a time and were camped in a dry cave far back in the woods. One morning Monty was awakened by the sound of a gunshot. Woody came running into the cave. His face had lost its color and he looked like a man who had seen the devil. He started raving about some kind of monster bird.

"It's the biggest gol-darned bird I ever saw! Wings the size of farm gates. It's got long talony claws hanging down and makes a roaring sound like thunder in a rain barrel. I shot up at it but it didn't even flinch. We best stay holed up in here till it goes away. I just hope to heaven it don't decide to come in here after us!"

56

Monty grabbed his rifle and said he was going to have a look. Woody started pleading with him not to leave the safety of the cave but Monty, knowing his friend was sort of excitable by nature anyway, was curious to see what this giant bird business was all about. He slipped out of the cave and was gone awhile. Woody wondered if he'd ever see his hunting buddy again. It wasn't too long, though, before Monty stuck his head back into the mouth of the cave grinning.

"Why, Mayl, you old fool," he yelled, "that bird of yours ain't no monster. It's just what they call an air machine. Haven't you ever seen one?"

Woody said he'd heard of them before, but had never seen one.

"Well, I saw one just last year at the county fair," said Monty and he took Woody out to see the airplane as it flew around in the clear blue sky.

The fellow that owned the airplane was the son of a well-to-do doctor in Waynesburg. He was taking his girlfriend for a ride and showing her the sights. They were flying in easy, slow circles high up in the air and hadn't even noticed the two hunters. The engine made so much noise they never even knew Woody had taken a shot at them.

Just then, however, as the plane flew over, Monty felt something drip down on his cheek. He rubbed it off with his finger and tasted it. It was gasoline. Suddenly alarmed, Monty realized that his friend had hit the aircraft after all and had put a hole in its exposed gas tank. The fuel was streaming out and the boy and his girlfriend had no idea what was happening. Yelling didn't do any good, they couldn't hear above the roar of the airplane's engine. Something had to be done and done quick!

57

Monty then remembered that they had had some corn-on-the-cob for supper the evening before. He ran back into the cave and fetched one of the corncobs. With his pocket knife he whittled a bullet from the cob, just the right size for his old muzzle-loading rifle. He put a charge of powder down the barrel and tamped the cob-bullet down on top of it. It was a bright day and he was forced to squint. But as the plane flew over, his sharp eyes spied the hole in the gas tank. Keeping his aim steady, Monty slowly squeezed the double-set trigger. BANG!

A perfect shot!

The cob bullet hit the hole in the tank and plugged it good. *Now that was a good shot!*

## Ruff Winds

Sometimes the wind gets up around Ruff Creek like the Devil is fanning himself to stay cool. It'll blow for days on end until every loose shingle and unlatched barn door is tore loose. One time, after a particularly bad spell of strong wind, Ray received the store's telephone bill in the mail. It was for $285.25! Ray was stunned. He seldom called anywhere far away. He figured there must be some mistake, maybe one of the telephone company's computers was on the fritz. He called them up to sort it out but was told that the high bill was a result of the unusually strong winds.

"You see, Mr. Stockdale," the customer representative said, "the wind blew so hard that it stretched all the telephone lines out a good bit. So, you see, *all the calls you made to your neighbors last month wound up being long-distance and we had to charge you for them.*"

58

Another time Ray took his family over to Carmichaels to the drive-in theater. The movie that was playing was a Western that they'd been looking forward to seeing. After paying, they parked the car and put the speaker through the window while the kids went for hot dogs and cokes. They were all settled in for a good time when that Greene County wind got up and the movie people had to give them their money back. They had no choice. *The trouble was that the movie picture kept blowing off the screen!*

## *Big Paul Bunyan*

At the store one day, Kissy Davin told some youngsters a story about the legendary logger, Paul Bunyan. He started out by informing them that ol' Paul wasn't like ordinary men. No sir. For one thing, the giant would work day and night cutting timber for two weeks solid without sleeping. Then, when he did rest, he'd sleep for five full days at a time. Kissy reckoned it had something to do with his considerable size. Paul's ox, Babe, was known to do the same thing.

One time, back when the country around Ruff Creek was a wilderness, a bunch of loggers from Canada slipped down into western Pennsylvania to cut timber. Of course the law didn't allow it but there were too few folks around to catch them. Their leader was a tough French-Canadian character named Claude Dumond and he had a crew of about sixty men working for him. They set up a saw mill along the river and then found a nice round mountain full of tall trees to clear. All day long the men sweat over their cross-cut saws and swung their double-headed axes felling the timber.

59

They finished just as it was getting dark and stacked the logs up in one enormous pile. Dog-tired, they threw their blankets on the hard ground and went to sleep.

When they awoke in the morning, they were greatly surprised to find that all the trees on the mountain had grown up again overnight. In all their days, they'd never seen anything like it! They reckoned the soil in Greene County was the richest in all the world if it could grow a full-size tree in one night. They spent the second day cutting down all the new trees and stacking them up alongside the logs from the day before. Again night came on and the men went to sleep after singing some old songs and swapping tales. In the morning it was the same incredible story all over. Every single tree had grown up again during the night, their tall trunks towering up into the sky. This made the superstitious loggers as nervous as cats in a roomfull of rocking chairs. They began to believe that the mountain was haunted somehow. Nothing else seemed to explain the way trees could grow so fast. Claude had trouble making the men stay on the mountain another day. He cajoled and threatened the rough loggers until they picked up their tools and started in again cutting the new timber. When they were finally done, they had three impressive piles of logs to show for all their work. Since none of the men would sleep another night on the mountain, Claude ordered the logs rolled down to the river where they could be floated to the saw mill. But the piles were so large and heavy, ten men with long poles couldn't get them to budge. So Claude took three kegs of black powder and placed one under each stack of logs. He ran some powder along the ground for a fuse and put a match to it.

There was a deafening explosion and the logs flew up into the air and began rumbling down the mountainside. But then the ground itself began shaking under their feet. They thought in terror that they had set off an earthquake! Stumbling and cursing, the frightened men ran for their lives.

When the loggers had at last gotten clear of the mountain, they looked back to see what had happened. What they had taken for a mountain had, in fact, only been big Paul Bunyan's face. He'd been sleeping and the trees they had been cutting down weren't trees at all. *They were only Paul's whiskers growing back again each night!*

## Gib Morgan's Deep Well

Kissy also tells about a real character named Gib Morgan who lived back before the turn of the century. He was a "wildcatter" and worked in the oil fields of western Pennsylvania and West Virginia drilling new oil wells. He had a fellow working for him named Fatty Walls. Fatty was notoriously lazy. They said he'd drive over a bump just to knock the ash off his cigar.He was what was called a "doodle-bugger". His job was to find oil under the ground by means of a "doodle-bug", a contraption that worked somewhat like the divining rod that's used to locate water. He was the best in the business, when he was of a mind to work. Gib and Fatty had been together for many years. Fatty would go out and find the oil and then it was Gib's job to take over and do the drilling.

One time Fatty was down in Greene County and he

61

found a place up in the woods where his doodle-bug started jumping like a native trout on a light line. Fatty knew the ground underneath was bound to be chock-full of black oil. He went and told his partner about it and a week later Gib hauled in a big steam drilling rig and set it up over the spot. The crew built a stout wooden derrick, tall enough to handle the drilling tools, and Gib commenced to work. The old-time drills worked pretty much like a farmer using a spud bar to dig a posthole. The drill bit was connected to a long, heavy steel bar. The bar was then lifted high up in the air by a cable attached to the steam engine and dropped, making a hole in the ground. The process was called "punching in a well".

Gib worked on the well until they were down 800 feet but he still hadn't struck oil. To make matters worse, he'd run into solid bedrock that, try as he might, he couldn't get through. For two whole weeks, his crew drilled on that tough rock but only managed nine inches. Gib felt as frustrated as a brood-hen sitting on a wooden egg. Fatty, however, assured him that there was oil to be found if he kept on.

"If you can get through that rock, somehow" said the Doodle-bugger, "why, you'll have more oil than you'll know what to do with. You'll be on easy street, I'm sure of it!" Fatty had never been wrong before and Gib was determined to see it through.

There was a circus touring around the county just then and it was set up just outside of Carmichaels. Its main attraction was an act billed as "The Human Cannonball" The circus had exciting, colorful posters in all the stores. It showed a man in a silver suit and leather helmet being shot out of a cannon and landing in a big net. This gave Gib an idea. He went down one morning to the fairgrounds and asked "cannonball" if he could rent his cannon for a day.

Gib then hired a team of horses and hauled the heavy cannon up into the woods to the drilling rig. He got the thing inside the derrick pointing straight down the 800-foot hole. He loaded it with three kegs of black powder, more powder than had ever been used in it before. A drill bit was placed in the muzzle of the gun, attached to a cable running up to the wheel at the top of the derrick. Gib then ran a long cord away from the cannon. When he was ready, he gave the cord a tug and the cannon fired. It made a roar like a hundred 4th of Julys! The air filled with clouds of black, sulphur-smelling smoke. Echoes from the blast could be heard for miles around.

Just as Gib had planned, the drill bit went screaming down the hole and, *crack*, it split the bedrock in two. But he'd put way too much powder in the cannon. After piercing the rock, the drill bit kept right on going down into the earth until the cable played out. Then, with a mighty jerk, the cannon, steam engine, derrick and all were pulled down into the hole after it. The driller's eyes stood out so far he could have hung his coat on them! There was nothing left but a black hole in the ground and some singed grass.

Then one of the men from the drilling crew came running up to Gib. "Oh, boss, it's terrible!"

"Don't tell me!" answered the driller in despair. "I've lost my good drilling rig and everything."

"No, that's not the worst part," continued the distraught man. "You know how lazy old Fatty is? Well, he'd slipped into the doghouse of the derrick to take a short nap. Now he's gone down the hole with everything else!"

This was awful news for Gib. He ran over to the top of the hole and, cupping his hands to his mouth, yelled, "F-a-t-t-y, you down there?"
There was no answer. Gib started back home feeling terrible. He'd worked with Fatty for so many years and now he was gone  But later, when Gib had been home an hour or so, there was a knock on the door. It was a fellow from the Western Union Telegraph office. He had a telegram for Gib.
*It was from Fatty! In China!*
It said he'd brought in the biggest oil well that ever was and was selling oil to the Chinamen. Said if Gib was ever in the neighborhood, he should stop by for a visit.

## The Boy Who Told Tall Tales

The Smith boy, Jimmy, was seven years old and he told the most fantastic tall tales anyone around Ruff Creek had ever heard. They weren't lies to hurt anyone or get himself out of trouble.  He just had an active imagination and loved to make up all kinds of yarns. Most folks seemed to enjoy these creations and encouraged him. The local minister, however, where Jimmy went to church, was concerned. He called Jimmy's parents into his office one Sunday morning before the worship service.
"I've heard about the fanciful, made-up stories Jimmy tells I think we should get him to stop. We're charged, after all, with teaching young people to be upright and truthful members of society. Why, from what I've heard, there's not a bit a truth in any of the stories your son tells."

64

The parents said they didn't think it was right to punish the little fellow since the stories seemed harmless and well-intentioned.

"I know," agreed the preacher,"but I've got an idea that might work. I'll tell Jimmy a totally incredible tale. When he sees a grown-up, a preacher, telling such nonsense, he'll see how foolish it is and feel embarrassed. He'll give up telling these stories then."

The parents weren't so sure they understood this logic but they respected the minister and would give it a try. After the service, they brought little Jimmy into the office. The preacher looked very impressive in his long black and purple robes.

"Jimmy, the most amazing thing happened here last Thursday night during choir practice." the minister started. "We were all up in the front of the church singing a hymn when the doors burst open and the biggest black bear you ever saw came running down the center isle. He was being chased by an itty-bitty brown dog, no bigger than both your hands. We ran for the choir room and, just as I was closing the door, I saw that enormous, fierce bear turn on that little dog. I shut the door, I couldn't stand to watch. We could hear loud barking and growling and I figured it was the end of that poor little dog. Then everything got quiet. I carefully pushed the door open and do you know what I saw? There was that little dog, wagging his tail, and not a scratch on him. But the front of the church was covered with black fur and bones where that little dog had tore that bear to pieces!"

"Now, Jimmy," said the minister gravely, "do you really believe that story?"

"Why, I sure do." said the boy excitedly. *"That was my little dog!"*

65

# CHAPTER FOUR

# Dogs, Horses, Mules, and Raccoon-Hunting Monkeys

*A reasonable amount o' fleas is good fer a dog - keeps him from broodin' over being a dog.* - Edward Westcott

## A Well-Trained Dog

Besides running the Ruff Creek General Store, Ray Stockdale's other love is raising and training fine hunting dogs. He excels at this vocation and his dogs have earned quite a reputation over the years. He carries a line of quality dog foods and supplies and it is not unusual to find someone who has driven a long ways to trade at his store or to purchase one of his superior dogs.

One time a man from West Virginia came to look over some of Ray's dogs. A fine year-old female named "Sally" caught his eye but, despite Ray's claims, he was somewhat skeptical about her merits.

"What you say she can do, and what she really can do, may be two different things, " said the fellow knowingly. "Before I hand over my hard-earned money for her, I want a demonstration."

Ray was obliging and he took the man and the dog with him up into the woods. Sally ran ahead of them for a time until she struck a track. She was off like the wind. The two men jogged after her but she was soon out of sight. The young dog had a good strong voice and they could hear her bellowing far away. Suddenly all was quiet.

"Well," said the West Virginian, with some satisfaction, "reckon your dog's lost the track."

Ray didn't answer. He just stood still as Sunday morning listening. One minute, two minutes, five minutes passed when, just as suddenly, they both heard Sally barking again far over on the other side of the valley.

"See, " said Ray proudly, "that dog never lost the track. *She was just crossing posted land.*"

## Two Mean Dogs

Some years ago out in the western end of Greene County down next to West Virginia, there lived an old man named Silas McGraw. He lived by himself so far up a holler that they had to pump the sunshine in. He didn't care at all for strangers snooping around his place so he kept him a dog that could outsnarl the Devil himself. Many a poor hunter lost a year or two off his life after having a run-in with this vicious creature. The dog's name was Gravel-Gut. He was stronger than a bulldog, faster than a greyhound, bigger than a Great Dane, and had the temperament of a pit-bull. Everyone in that part of the county knew where Silas' place was and stayed clear of it for fear of that dog.

Not far away, up on Wind Ridge someplace, a fellow named Buckshot Johnson lived and he was just as anxious as Silas was to keep any and all trespassers off his land. He claimed his own dog was the meanest dog as ever lived. He'd christened the creature Bloody Tooth, after the dog's successful tangle with a rash bill collector when he wasn't much more than a pup. His long teeth were sharp as daggers and his eyes burned like two coals from Hell. His growl would turn a grown man's legs to jelly and his bite was worse than his bark. Buckshot only fed the dog on raw meat so he'd always have a taste for fresh blood.

One time, Silas was needing a used rear end for his '54 Chevy truck. He heard Buckshot might have one and went over to see about it. He decided to take Gravel-Gut along with him. Unfortunately, he never thought to warn Buckshot of his visit to make sure the other dog was chained up. Ol' Bloody-Tooth was laying

under the porch when he caught sight of Silas and his dog coming up the bottom towards the house. Like lightning, Bloody-Tooth started for them. Since Gravel-Gut was such a dangerous dog himself, Silas had him on a stout leash made from 12 oz. harness leather. When Silas' dog saw Bloody-Tooth coming on like murder on four legs, his own killing instinct reached a fever pitch. He lunged on the leash so hard and sudden-like that it snapped like a daisy chain. Ignoring Silas' yells, Gravel-Gut went tearing straight for the other dog. The sprinting dogs looked like two big steam locomotives racing towards each other at full tilt on the same track. The closer they came, the more their gaping mouths opened wider and wider. Their yellow teeth glistened and white foam streamed from their snarling lips. When they finally came together at a full run, each dog was so determined to kill that *they completely swallowed each other up and just disappeared!*
They were certainly two mean dogs!

## The Old Horse's Retirement

A farmer named Blaine Martin who lived over near Nineveh owned a fine old workhorse named "Major". The horse had given many years of faithful service on the farm but had developed a pair of sores on his back. One was where the heavy collar rubbed near the base of his neck and the other was where the backstrap crossed over. Because of the animal's considerable age, the sores wouldn't heal over but continued to fester. It was painful for the creature and Blaine refused to put him in harness anymore. Neighbors advised selling the useless workhorse at the stock auction but Blaine wouldn't hear of it. He couldn't bear the thought of old Major winding up in some can of dog food somewhere.

So one day, figuring the horse had paid his dues and deserved a dignified retirement, Blaine decided just to turned him loose on his farm. Swinging the big farm gate open, he watched as the old horse slowly made his way up the holler. The farm was over 800 acres and Blaine didn't see the horse again after that. He believed the animal must have finally died and the buzzards had taken care of him.

Some years later Blaine's boy was back from college for the Thanksgiving Day holidays. Father and son decided to do some deer hunting and Opening Day found them, rifles in hand, crossing a small meadow at the far end of the farm. As they worked their way up towards the ridge, the boy stopped all of a sudden and tugged on his father's coat sleeve. He pointed ahead to a small patch of woods. Blaine couldn't believe what he saw. The trees appeared to be moving! It wasn't the wind or anything else he could explain. It looked, for all the world, as if the trees were walking around on their own. Blaine was determined to find out what was going on.

Flicking the safety off his rifle, the farmer and his son started up towards the woods. It was then that they saw Major. The old workhorse was still alive after all those years. But that wasn't all! When the acorns had been dropping in the fall sometime back, one must have landed in each of the two sores on the horse's back. Both had taken root and sprouted.

There were now two full-sized oak trees growing out of the back of that horse!

71

Now Blaine wasn't college educated but he knew a thing or two and never let an opportunity go to waste. When he'd gotten over the shock of seeing the old horse again, and in such an altered state, the farmer took hold of the horse's mane and led him back down to the barn. He put a halter on and tied him to a fence post. Fetching his chain saw, Blaine then cut the front tree down, leaving about a foot of stump still standing. He got enough wood from that one tree when he'd hauled it to the sawmill to frame a new roof for his tractor shed. He never cut down the other tree, though, which was hard for his son to understand. He didn't see how his father could get the horse into the barn with all the branches sticking way out. But Blaine had his reasons. The next summer, around about August, when it got so hot and dry that all the creeks dried up, Blaine would ride around his farm on old Major. He'd sit on the stump with the oak tree swaying behind him, keeping the sun off. He kept that horse for many years. Best horse he ever owned.

## The Stubborn Mule

A fellow from Uniontown came over to Holbrook to see a horsedealer about purchasing a mule. The dealer's name was Denzil and he had several mules and horses rounded up in a pasture for the man to look at.
"Well, mister," said the dealer, "what exactly are you looking for?"
The man replied he wanted a strong animal that wasn't allergic to hard work.
"Well, I've got just the one for you, then," said the dealer, as he pointed to a big brown mule at the far end

of the field. "Only thing, though, he's awfully mule-headed."

"That's no problem," said the man confidently. "I can handle any stubborn mule alive. What's important is if he's fit to work." They went out into the field and the man checked the mule's teeth and legs and agreed to buy him. Denzil put a halter on the animal and hooked a long lead to it. He started leading him back towards the barn. The field was surrounded by a fancy board fence and, as they came up to the gate, the mule walked right into it with his head before Denzil could open it.

"Why, that mule's blind!" said the man indignantly.

"No, he's not blind at all," said the dealer. *"He just don't give a damn!"*

## Argil's Old Mule

Up the road from Ruff Creek in Plum Sock is Argil Bailey's place. He lives and works the same 80-acre farm where he was born and raised. He had an old mule one time named Jake who helped him with his farming. The mule had worked in the coal mines and was so accustomed to that kind of work that, come five o'clock of an evening, no matter where he was, or what job of work he was doing, he'd stop and wait to be taken to the barn and his feed. Nothing could make him keep on. This often annoyed Argil but, try as he might, he couldn't persuade the stubborn creature to change his ways.

One very hot summer's day Argil was plowing some land that he'd rented from another farmer several miles from his own place. It was so hot out that the

73

birds were using pot holders to pull worms out of the ground. The scorching sun was beating down on the farmer and the mule until both were drenched with sweat. Argil had several furrows left to plow when the mule's "quitting time" arrived. Jake stopped and wouldn't take another step. Knowing from past experience it was useless to fight the dumb creature, Argil unhitched the plow and started for home, leading the mule.

As soon as they started down the state road, a fancy brand-new convertible came along and pulled up next to them. It was Carter Simpson, Argil's neighbor.

"Howdy, Argil," he said, "looks like you two have been working pretty hard."

"It's the heat that wears you out mostly." answered the farmer.

"Well, what do you think of my new car? It's a beauty, don't you think?" the neighbor then remarked. He was on his way home after picking up his new car from the Ford dealership in Waynesburg.

"Why, it sure is something, alright." agreed Argil, looking the car over and nodding his head.

"It's the convertible business that's the best part," went on Carter. "Come on, I'll give you a ride home and you can see how nice it is on a hot day."

"Well, what about my mule?" asked Argil.

"Why shoot, he can come along too!" answered Carter. He then leaned over and opened the door and Jake climbed into backseat. The old mule's head shot high up in the air and his front hooves hung over the front seat. Argil then got in and off they went.

The new car rode along so smooth it was like sitting in a rocking chair. The cool wind blowing through the open-top car felt wonderful. Jake had a big grin on his face and his mane was rippling in the breeze. In no time the sweat on both Argil and Jake had dried and they were having a great time.

"Nothing like it, is there?" yelled Carter, with obvious delight. "Why, the trick is the faster you go, the cooler you get!" In no time they came even with the long drive up to Argil's farm. The neighbor stopped his car and let them out.

"Well, thanks for the ride." said Argil.

"Glad to do it," replied Carter. "Remember now what I told you. The faster you go the cooler you get!" With that, he drove off.

The old man started leading Jake up the lane but then decided that the mule should at least carry him. He climbed up on his back and then had another idea. Leaning over, he whispered in the mule's ear.

"Remember what Carter said, the faster you go, the cooler you get!" Argil hit the mule on the flank with the reins and they started to jog down the lane. "Come on, Jake," encouraged Argil, "faster you go, the cooler you get!" The mule broke out of a trot and into a run. He came tearing up the lane with the old man on his back slapping him with the reins and yelling, "faster you go, the cooler you get, faster you go, the cooler you get!"

They got almost to the barn when the heat and exertion took its toll. The old animal's heart gave out and he suddenly collapsed under the farmer. The poor mule lay on the road, dead as a creek rock, while the old man worked to get out from under him. Just then Argil's wife came out on the porch.

"What in the world happened to Jake?" she yelled.

"I'm not exactly sure." replied the farmer somewhat confused. *"Reckon he just froze to death."*

## Raccoon-Hunting Monkey

There's a farmer up on the ridge above Ruff Creek who loves to hunt raccoons. His name is Rory and he owns several good coon-hounds. Most of his spare time he spends chasing his dogs over the hills of Greene County with his neighbor, Melvin, another avid coon hunter.

One day as Rory was reading the back section of a sporting magazine, he saw a classified ad that caught his eye. It read:

RACCOON-HUNTING MONKEYS FOR SALE
$100 each
P.O. Box 1334  Los Angeles, California

Now Rory couldn't imagine what a 'raccoon-hunting' monkey could be but his curiosity was aroused. Several days passed and the thought preyed on his mind like a shred of meat stuck in his teeth. Finally he gave in, wrote out a check, and sent it off. He figured it was worth the money just to discover what the monkey-business was all about and have done with it.

About two weeks later Rory was in the house when he heard a car-horn sounding. He went out on the porch and saw the mailman's car at the end of his drive.

"We've got a crate for you down at the Post Office," he yelled up to Rory. "You'd better get down there right away and pick it up. There's something alive inside it, you can hear it scrambling around. It's got Millie pretty upset."

It took Rory a few minutes to remember what he'd sent for. Then it finally came to him. It was the

76

raccoon-hunting monkey! He jumped in his pickup truck and drove down to the Post Office. He loaded the large crate into the back and headed for home. He then took a bar and pried the lid open.

Inside was a two-foot tall, brown monkey with long skinny arms and an S-shaped tail. He had on a red leather collar and seemed as well-mannered as Shirley Temple. Also in the box was a leather leash and an instruction book. It told all about the monkey and, as Rory thumbed through it, he got excited. He called his hunting buddy, Melvin, and told him to come over at dusk that evening to do some hunting. Rory had something very special to show him.

"What in the world do you have there?" asked Melvin, when he saw the unusual creature.

"Why, it's a monkey," said Rory with pride.

"I know it's a monkey!" exclaimed Melvin. "What I want to know is, what are you going to do with it?"

Rory said he'd see soon enough. They took two of Rory's dogs and started up into the woods. Each man had a carbide light on his hat to see with, like the ones coal miners used to use, and Rory led the monkey along on his leash. Soon the dogs got the scent and were off. Their hearty barking filled the quiet night as the two men ran after them. The little monkey had no trouble keeping up with them on his little legs.

When the hunters at last reached the dogs, they were excitedly barking and jumping up at the foot of a big sugar maple. It was dark as pitch and neither man could catch sight of the raccoon up in the tree. Then Rory unhooked the monkey from the leash. The little fellow sat back on his haunches and held out his tiny hand. Melvin watched in amazement as Rory took a small, nickel-plated .22 revolver from his pocket and gave it to the monkey. The monkey then scrambled up the maple like a 4th of July rocket. He wasn't up in the tree thirty seconds when there was a shot. The poor raccoon came falling out of the tree and landed with a thud on the leaves. He was stone dead, shot between the eyes. The monkey came down the tree and politely handed the pistol back to Rory. Melvin was thunderstruck. He'd never ever seen anything like it!

"Do you think we could go out again tomorrow night and take the monkey along?" Melvin wanted to know on their way home.

"No, I can't," said Rory. "Wednesday evenings me and the wife go to church. But you can borrow the monkey, if you want."

So the next night Melvin took the monkey and his own dogs out hunting. But around three o'clock in the morning, Rory received a telephone call at home, waking him from a deep sleep.

"Rory, what kind of fool monkey is that, anyhow?" Melvin yelled over the phone. Rory had never heard his friend so upset before and he struggled to collect his wits.

"Calm down, for goodness sake, and tell me what happened?" he said.

"I took that monkey along with me," Melvin went on, "but my dogs had trouble finding a track. Finally they got on to something and me and the monkey chased after them. We found the hounds at the foot of a sycamore but I couldn't see any coon. So I gave the monkey the pistol and he went up the tree, just like last night. He was up there five minutes, ten minutes, fifteen minutes, and nothing happened. Then, after about a half hour, the monkey comes back down the tree. When he hits the ground, he stands up on his hind legs and shoots both of my dogs straight through the head. They were my best dogs he killed!"

Rory could hear the anger and hurt in Melvin's voice and he said as gently as he could, "It's all my fault, Melvin, I'll do what I can to make it up to you. I read the instructions but I didn't think to warn you. It says plainly that *if there is anything that monkey hates worse than raccoons, it's lying dogs!*"

## The Mother-in-Law and the Mule

Murray's mother-in-law came to visit only twice a year. Of course each time she stayed six months. One day as she was out in the barn, she happened to walk behind Murray's red mule, Ajax. The animal suddenly, without warning, lashed out with his hind legs and struck the old woman on the side of the head. She died instantly.

The next day they had the old woman's wake at the house. Murray's neighbor, Delbert, put on his Sunday suit and went to pay his respects. As he neared the house, he saw a tremendous number of cars and trucks. They were parked all around the house and down both sides of the long driveway. As he entered the house, he noticed Murray in the midst of a large group of men. Delbert drew his friend aside.

"Why, I had no idea your mother-in-law was so well liked." he said.

"She wasn't," was the son-in-law's reply. *"These folks are here to buy my red mule!"*

79

# CHAPTER FIVE

# Kissy Davin

# Master Storyteller

*A storyteller is someone who has a good memory and hopes others don't.*

*He's someone who tells the truth about something that never happened.*

## Kissy's First Job

The first real job Kissy had when he was a young man was as a brakeman on the railroad. The line he worked for hauled freight, mostly coal and farm products, and also provided limited passenger service. It wasn't a wealthy company, by any means, and often got by with hand-me-down equipment from other more prosperous railroads.

One time Kissy was riding back in the caboose with an old veteran nicknamed, "Walker". The brakeman had received his name because of his skill in negotiating the dangerous catwalks that ran along the top of the swaying cars. Every five minutes or so, the old brakeman would take out his big, key-wound railroad watch and flip open the lid. He'd get up then and pull a long section of steel pipe out from under his seat. Leaving the caboose and stepping carefully over the coupling onto the next car, he'd climb the narrow ladder attached to the end of the old wooden boxcar. When he got on top, he'd hit the roof of the boxcar three good licks with the heavy pipe. Just made it roar. Then he'd simply climb back down, return to the caboose, replace the pipe under his seat, sit down and light his pipe, and look out the window. He never said a word.

Kissy was just eaten up with curiosity to know what it was all about. He'd never heard of such a thing being part of railroad work. But as he was new on the job, he was too embarrassed to ask, thinking it would make him appear stupid.

This went on a dozen times or more, always the same, until Kissy couldn't take it any longer. "What in Sam Hill are you doing, Walker?" Kissy finally asked.

Walker looked back at the younger man with the wisdom born of long experience and said, "This here is an unusual case, Kissy. I don't reckon you'd know much about it. You see," continued the older man, "we're running some pretty old equipment on this line. Take that boxcar, for example. It's only rated for ten tons."

"I know that," said Kissy impatiently, "but why are you hitting the top of it with that pipe and making such a racket?"

"Hold on now and I'll get to that," the brakeman answered. "You see, the thing is we've got 20 tons of chickens in that car. *I've got to keep half of 'em in the air all the time.*"

## The Bad Drought

After his experience with railroading, Kissy got married and settled down. He bought a nice piece of property in Ruff Creek and went into the farming business. He had a few good years and, then, there was a terrible drought. It barely rained a drop from May up into August. First the creeks dried up, then the springs, and finally the well itself. There wasn't a drop of water in it, it was bone-dry. To make matters worse, Kissy's mother-in-law got sick about then. He went to the drug store in Waynesburg and bought some medicine for her. They were great big yellow pills. Only when he got back home, he realized there wasn't any water on the place for her to swallow them with.

Now Kissy had a team of Percheron draft horses. They were large animals, with hooves the size of #10 frying pans. He harnessed them up and hooked a stout

83

log-chain to the double trees. The other end of the chain he wrapped around the top of the well. He then gave the traces a snap and the old horses dug down and pulled so hard that they snaked the well clean out of the ground. Then Kissy fired up the gasoline-powered Maytag washing machine. It made a racket like someone shooting a machine gun. He pulled the lever and started the rubber wringers turning. He then passed the well through them, squeezing out three full glasses of water from that dried-up well.

His mother-in-law was able to take her pills but Kissy was in a quandary as to what to do with the well. It had gotten twisted and maimed so bad, it wouldn't fit back down into the ground. But Kissy was always an opportunist. He took down his crosscut saw and cut the well into two-foot sections. It had been a deep well and he got quite a few. These he sold to local farmers for post holes, at a dollar a crack, and made a good bit of money on the deal.

Although Kissy had solved one headache, he had another one to work on. With so little rain, the grass had turned as brown and tough as shoe leather. It still had nutrients in it but the cattle refused to eat it, on account of the color mostly. The poor animals kept losing weight until they were practically skin and bones. Farmers throughout the county were forced to sell off their stock at only a few cents a pound.

Kissy was determined not to take this route. He remembered seeing an ad for some surplus W. W. II Air Force equipment. He hunted it up and it gave him an idea. He wrote out a check and sent it to the company selling the goods. When the crate arrived, he tore it open and found what he'd ordered, one hundred pairs of green-tinted aviation glasses.

He put a pair on each one of his hundred head of cattle. They looked mighty peculiar but it sure did the trick. With those glasses on, the old brown grass appeared green and luscious. That fooled the cattle and they started eating it. It wasn't long until they'd fattened right up. That way Kissy was able to keep his stock through till the next year when they fetched a good price at the market.

## The Talking Contest

Over the years folks have often asked Kissy how he came to be such a consummate storyteller. His response is that he's come by it honestly, being descended from a long, distinguished line of tale-spinners. To make his point, he'll launch into a funny story about his father, Ralie Davin, whose prowess as a great talker was well-known. As a young man, Ralie served with Pershing in the American Expeditionary Forces that fought in Europe during WWI. He served in a front-line unit and saw some heavy action.

One time, while on leave from the front, Ralie was recuperating in a small French village far from the trenches and constant shelling. It was morning and he was enjoying a glass of cognac with some army buddies when he noticed, at another table, a French captain regaling a group of soldiers with some long-winded tale. They were laughing and slapping their knees one minute and serious as Baptist preachers the next. Of course Ralie couldn't catch a word of what was said, not knowing the language, but he was highly intrigued by the officer's animated voice and gestures. He called

85

the waiter over and asked about the fellow.

"Oh, but of course," replied the waiter with pride. "That is the famous Jean-Pierre Deschenes. He is the greatest talker in France, in the whole world!"

This information awakened Ralie's competitive nature. He listened to the captain awhile longer and then said to his friends with great certainty, " Why, he's not such a hot talker even if I can't understand a word of it. There's lots of fellows back in Ruff Creek could top him. I could do it myself!"

Well, one thing led to another. The Americans championed Ralie while the French soldiers staunchly defended their man. Numerous boasts and challenges were thrown back and forth until a contest was decided upon. Since neither of the key figures understood the other's language, they agreed to a set of simple rules which would determine who, in fact, was the best talker. Whichever one could talk for the longest time, without stopping for any reason, outlasting the other, would be declared the winner! Bets were placed by the soldiers on the outcome but, to the contestants, their sole motivation was defending their own professional dignity and national honor.

Two straight-back chairs were drawn up and the two men sat facing each other, so close that their knees almost touched. Large tumblers of water were provided near to hand. The tension was thick in the room as the waiter, with great solemnity, popped a cork from some champagne to signal the start.

The Frenchman had a wonderfully deep voice and spoke with great feeling. The fact that Ralie couldn't understand what he said would have no bearing on the outcome of the contest. The championship would simply go to the talker who was the most long-winded.

Ralie started off, as he often did when passing the time with a neighbor back home in Ruff Creek, discussing the important topic of weather. He discussed how someone could tell if it was going to rain, how hard a winter to expect, and when it would stay dry enough to put up hay. That got him onto farming which, after a bit, led to the new government farm bill. This, of course, meant politics and Ralie spent several hours alone on this weighty subject. He discussed everything from the last presidential election to his plans to run for township supervisor when he got home. By this point, Ralie was just getting warmed up and enjoying himself. He took a big swallow of water and broached one of his favorite topics, hunting. He elaborated on this subject in depth far into the night and his knowledge was inexhaustible.

For his part, the Frenchman held up well in the early going but, as the hours rolled by, the effort took its toll. His face became haggard, his tongue thick, and his throat hoarse with fatigue. Slowly the group around the talkers began to thin out as the soldiers stretched out on the floor and fell asleep. It was well past midnight, with the sky black and the moon rising, when the last spectator nodded off. The combatants, each stubborn and determined to win, had been at it non-stop for over 15 1/2 hours and were still talking!

When morning came the soldiers began to stir. They were stiff from their hard beds. The bright early sun poured in through the windows of the cafe and made them squint as they looked about. What they saw revealed, without question, who had won the contest. Down on the floor of the restaurant was the French captain, stone cold dead, with Ralie leaning over him, *whispering in his ear.*

## Kissy and the Hunters

One fall Kissy was moving some hay on his farm. He was using a large wagon and team to do the hauling and, when he got down to the state road, he stopped to open the gate. It was hunting season and two city fellows had their Blazer parked next to the road. They'd apparently been out all day long but hadn't killed anything. They were in a sour mood and, when they saw the old farmer, they decided to have some fun. They walked over just as Kissy was swinging the gate open.

"Hey, old man," said one of the hunters, "you ever done any dancing?" He was holding a semi-automatic rifle and had it pointed at Kissy's feet.

"No, but I always wanted to!" was Kissy's reply.

The city fellow started shooting and the farmer started jumping, the bullets ricochetting off the gravel at his feet. Kissy's poor feet were just flying and the two hunters were laughing like fools. But the rifle finally ran out of bullets and, as the hunter started fumbling around in his pockets for more, Kissy moved over next to his wagon. He quietly slid his double-barrel 12-gauge out from under the seat where he always kept it and leveled it at the two hunters. Looking down the business end of the shotgun, the two city slickers got sober in a hurry. Kissy let them sweat for a few minutes without saying a word. Then he spoke to the fellow with the empty rifle in a casual sort-of-way.

"Son, you ever kissed the back end of an old horse before?"

"No," said the man with feeling, "but I always wanted to!"

88

## Kissy's Adventure

One day Kissy and some of the regulars were at the store swapping yarns about the close calls they'd had. "I'd had me a job one time with United States Forest Service out in Idaho," Kissy began."One morning I was on my way to relieve a fellow ranger up in a fire tower in the mountains when, suddenly, out of nowhere, a big, mean grizzly started after me. Well, I took to my heels. But that bear was a powerful runner. No matter how fast I ran, he just kept gaining on me. I could feel the beast's hot breath blowing down the back of my neck, he was that close. Finally I had no choice but to clamber up a tall spruce tree and hope the bear would leave me alone. The bear pawed at the tree trunk with his sharp claws awhile and growled up at me. I don't mind telling you fellows, I was never so scared before in all my life! Then the grizzly gave me a queer look, as much to say, I'll be back, and he ran off through the trees. Well, I stayed right where I was. I was just frozen with fear. But soon he came back again carrying two large beavers by their tails, one in each paw. The bear placed them critters at the foot of the spruce and they commenced doing what beavers do best. They gnawed away at the trunk of that tree with their sharp teeth like two 20-inch Homelite chainsaws. Them beavers kept at it for more than an hour with me sitting up there on top rocking back and forth and holding on for dear life. They finally chewed plum through the tree and the whole thing come down with a crash!"
"What'd the grizzly do to you then?" asked Charlie.
"Well, what do you think?," replied Kissy surprised.
*"He just ate me up, of course!"*

89

# CHAPTER SIX

# More Mountain Humor

*Humor, to a man, is like a feather pillow. The materials to make one are easy to come by and yet give great comfort.*
    - old Irish saying

*If you can laugh at yourself, you'll always be amused.*

## Three-Legged Chicken

A lawyer from Waynesburg was on his way to New Freeport, out in the western end of the county, to have an elderly client sign some papers. He turned off the main road and was driving down a narrow red-dog road when he suddenly noticed a small reddish-brown chicken running along by the side of his car. The chicken had three legs! The lawyer looked down at the speedometer and realized he was going 30 miles an hour. Never having heard of a chicken able to run so fast, he pressed down on the gas pedal and was soon bouncing down the road at 45 miles an hour. When he looked out the window, the little chicken was still running right along with the car. Determined to out-race the chicken, no matter what, the lawyer speeded up to 60. The car was tearing along with its tires throwing loose gravel and clouds of dirt to both sides. Satisfied the animal could never keep up, once more he looked out of his car window. The chicken was still there, close enough to spit on. The startled lawyer nearly ran off the road in surprise.

Just then they passed a farm and the chicken went racing up into the yard. The lawyer stopped his car and backed up. He could see twenty or more three-legged chickens pecking around in the yard. He got out of his car and started up to the house. He passed the barn and saw another dozen three-legged chickens roosting up on the rafters. He climbed the steps to the porch and knocked. Soon a farmer opened the screen door and asked him what he wanted.

The lawyer said, "I hope I'm not taking you from something but I happened to be passing your place and

noticed your unusual three-legged chickens. One of them was able to keep up with my car doing 60 miles an hour. I've been around some, but I've never seen anything like these birds. What's the story?"
"Well, you know how everybody loves a drumstick," the farmer said. "My brother and me have been doing some amateur experimenting up here, you know, crossing one breed of chicken with another. Well, we finally came up with these fellows. They seem to be thriving, don't you think?"
The lawyer agreed and said, "Well, how do they taste, this three-legged variety, I mean?"
But the farmer replied shaking his head, "Darned if I know, mister. *I can't even catch the fool things!*"

## *Judgement Day*

An old-time preacher came through Ruff Creek some years ago. He was afire with self-righteous enthusiasm and determined to spread the gospel throughout the land. He spent several days working on the boys down at the general store. The preacher put away numerous bags of potato chips and bottles of Coca-Cola but had little success winning converts. He decided to give up on the store crowd and direct his efforts to evangelizing folks out in the countryside.
One sunny day, while walking up a lonely country road, he spied an old man up on the porch of an old-fashioned farmhouse. The old fellow was sitting on a split-bottom chair, playing the fiddle. This encouraged the preacher, who figured that anyone who played that heathen instrument, was in need of salvation.
"Hey, brother, are you a Christian?" the preacher

93

yelled from the front gate.

Putting down the fiddle and pointing with his bow, the old man answered, "No, them Christians live about two mile up the road."

"That's not what I meant, old timer," responded the preacher, undaunted in his zeal. "Are you a lost soul?"

The farmer thought a bit and replied, "Well, young fellow, this is Greene County, ain't it? And this here is Mud Lick, last time I looked. No, don't reckon I'm lost."

The poor preacher was exasperated! He tried once more, "Look here, farmer, don't you know about Judgement Day?"

"When's that?" the old man wanted to know.

"Well, it could be tomorrow, or it could be next Saturday." replied the preacher.

The farmer then yelled back, "Well, whatever you do, don't tell my wife. *She'll want to go both days!*"

## *The Old Woman's Sleeping Potion*

As everybody knows, making and selling home made whiskey is illegal, if only because the government resents the fact that it can't collect taxes on it. Ever since the first settlers came into the mountains of western Pennsylvania, however, there have been independent souls who believe it is their natural right to cook up a little moonshine on the side. In one case, moonshine was a godsend to the Remsbach family.

Willard Remsbach's mother was getting on in years and was having trouble sleeping through the night. Doctor Knox was called to the house and, after examining the elderly woman, drew the son aside and said, "There's nothing wrong with your mother but old age, Will, and medical science can't do anything about that yet. There's no need to give her drugs, so I want you to try something for me." He told Will to give his mother about two-fingers worth of whiskey before she went to bed at night. "That'll help her get off to sleep and it's as good as anything I could give her."

"Oh, I couldn't do that!" said Will, rattled at the thought. "You don't understand, Doc. Ma is a strict three-times-a-week church-going Christian. She's never smoked, drank alcohol, or used a profane word in her whole life. Why, she'd never speak to me again if I offered her whiskey, no matter what the reason."

"Well then," the doctor replied confidentially, "we'll just have to trick the old girl. It's for her own good, after all. You've got a milk cow, don't you?"

Willard nodded and Dr. Knox continued, "Well, you get hold of some pure, A-number-one, 120 proof homemade whiskey. Old man Johnson's is the best and safest shine around these parts, by far. It's clear as spring water and practically tasteless. Pour some in the heated milk you give to your mother before she goes to bed at night. She'll never catch on and it'll help her to sleep." Will agreed somewhat reluctantly to the deception, not knowing what else to do.

The next evening, after milking, Will put some of the potent whiskey into his mother's warm milk. He gave it to her and she drank it down taking no apparent notice of the alcohol. In ten minutes she was snoring away and slept the whole night through without waking. In the morning, she appeared rested and happy.

For over three years the old woman drank her

95

doctored warm milk without comment and slept just fine. Then the old woman really began to fail and the doctor had to be called for again. Dr. Knox examined his patient and then spoke with Willard and his wife.

"I'm sorry, Will, but it doesn't look good. Most likely your mother won't make it through the night. I don't expect she'll have much pain, but you'd better go in and say your farewells." The doctor took his leave and Will and his wife went into the old woman's room. His mother looked pale and drawn, but at peace.

"Mama, do you know what's happening?" asked the distraught son.

"Yes, son, I'm getting ready to 'Cross Over Jordan'," answered the woman without fear.

"Is there anything you'd like to say before you leave us?" asked Will's wife.

"I've just one thing to say," answered the old woman feebly. *"Whatever you do, don't sell that cow!"*

## Politics

There's quite a lot of spirited competition between the Democrats and the Republicans around Ruff Creek, with the Democrats holding a decided edge in terms of numbers, at least. Of course, that's the name of the game when it comes election time in November.

Now John Reily is a Republican. His father and grandfather had been members of the Grand Old Party, so he comes by his political persuasion naturally. He's never had much use for 'them bleeding-heart Roosevelt Democrats', as he calls them.

One time, John had some tests run by his doctor when he hadn't been feeling quite up to snuff. The doctor told him that if the results came back negative, he'd be fine. If, on the other hand, they came back positive, there might not be anything the doctor could do and John had best get his affairs in order.

"Well, Doc," John replied, "if it comes to that, I'm going to join the Democratic party!"

The doctor, who'd known the old man for many years and was a staunch Republican himself, said in astonishment, "I just don't understand, John. You've been a loyal, straight-ticket, card-holding Republican all your life. Now, when you might not have long to live, you want to change over and become a worthless Democrat!"

"The way I got it figured, Doc," the old man shot back, *"better one of them should die than one of us!"*

Luckily, John's results came back negative and he's still voting Republican.

Dewey Shires, on the other hand, has always been a Democrat. He voted the straight Democratic ticket faithfully except just once. One afternoon Dewey was sitting down at the store when someone asked him why he'd recently quit working in the coal mines.

Dewey answered, "It was on account of the accident. I was working in a mine in Kirby and they had us working way back underground, about seven miles from the portal. Took over thirty minutes just to reach the face, to start with. Well, there was a young fellow working with me who was dumber than a box of rocks! Kept making mistakes. Finally he did something that brought the whole top down just behind where I was working. I was completely blocked in with tons of rock and slate. There was only a hole about a half-foot wide at the top of the cave-in. I got out my self-rescuer but I couldn't get it to work. I was getting desperate. The air was bad and I was feeling light-headed. That fool boy had gone for help but I knew they wouldn't reach me in time. I couldn't hope to clear away enough of the rock to get free before the air ran out, so I sat down with my back against the rib and waited for death. Then I began to see my life passing before my eyes. Saw when I was a kid in school, then later when I was in the service, and when I got married. Then I remembered voting for Ronald Reagan for president, the only time I ever voted for a Republican. I just couldn't stomach the Democratic ticket that year. Do you know what happened? As a long-time faithful Democrat, *I felt so small about voting that way, I was able to climb out through the half-foot hole and escape!* Never been in the mines a day since then."

Now, Lona Jean, Dewey's wife, doesn't belong to either political party. It's useless for volunteers canvassing votes around Ruff Creek to waste time on her, wouldn't do them any good. She's kept her eyes and ears open over the years and has her own ideas about politicians. When asked who she's intending to vote for, whether in a local, state-wide, or national race, she says, "I don't vote for any of 'em, *it encourages 'em!*"

## The Hen-pecked Husband

There was a farmer in Plum Sock, named Buell, who, although he wasn't a bigamist, had one wife too many. The woman he'd tied the knot with was of the opinion that there were only two things wrong with men: everything they said and everything they did. This covered a considerable bit of ground. This shrewish woman kept after Buell from morning to night, always telling him what to do and what not to do. The poor man didn't have a moment's peace from her constant demands and abuse.

Now Buell was one of them easy-to-get-along-with kind-of-fellows. He put up with the old woman's terrible nagging without complaint. His philosophy was that anyone can get used to hanging, if he hangs long enough.

There was one act of rebellion, however, that Buell clung to no matter what his wife said or did. And that was to go up to a beer joint in Pancake on Saturday nights and drink a few beers with his buddies. The old woman couldn't stand it. She'd threaten and pout and carry on terrible but the old man would go out all the same.

One day, Buell's wife was talking with her brother. "I swear, Emmett, if I can't break Buell of going up to that beer joint, they're going to have to put me in the penitentiary for murder!"

"Now, now, Marcie, don't get all worked up," her brother said. "I've got a sure-fire plan to make Buell give up his Saturday night gallivanting. Tell me, doesn't he always take that short-cut through the graveyard on his way home from the beer joint?"

Marcie said he did, with awakened interest.

"Well," Emmett went on, "you're awfully clever with a sewing machine. You make me up a devil's costume out of some red silky-type stuff. Put a long tail on it and little horny things up on top. I'll put it on and go up and hide in the graveyard. When Buell comes along, I'll jump out and scare the living daylights out of him. Why, he'll never again go to town on Saturday nights, if he thinks the devil's after him."

The old woman thought the idea was perfect and said

she wanted to tag along to see the old man get the fright of his life. That's the kind of woman she was. All week long she kept the old Singer treadle going clicketyclack. When Saturday evening finally arrived she had the costume all ready.

After supper that evening, Buell pushed back from the table and said, like it was the first time he'd ever thought of it. "It sure is a nice evening, think I'll just slip over to Pancake for a couple of hours."

Marcie replied, "Well, have a nice time."

This took the old man completely by surprise and he asked if she was feeling alright.

"I feel just fine," said the old woman, smiling. "You just go on and enjoy yourself. I'll see you later."

Buell wasted no time putting on his hat and coat. He figured he'd best get going, while the going was good.

As soon as he left, Marcie rang up Emmett and told him to hurry right over. Emmett arrived and put on the devil's outfit. He looked exactly like the pictures of Lucifer that he'd seen as a kid in the books at Sunday School. Reaching up into the chimney, Emmett collected some soot from the smoke shelf which he smeared on his face and hands. He looked awful, even gave Marcie a start.

When all was ready, the two conspirators went up to the cemetery. It was a cold damp night and they each had to scrunch down behind a small gravestone to keep hid. They waited a long time but Buell failed to show. The old woman's rheumatism began to act up and her temper started to rise. Her husband, it turned out, had decided to take full advantage of his wife's unaccustomed tolerance to stay a little longer and enjoy a few extra beers.

Finally, Buell made his way up the road, whistling an

100

old tune. He turned in at the gate of the cemetery and started to weave his way through the stone markers. Suddenly Emmett jumped out and let loose with a blood-curdling scream.

Backing up a little, Buell said in a puzzled voice, "Why, who the devil are you?"

Marcie's brother, in a fit of frustration, said, "Why, I am the Devil! Can't you see that, you old fool?" Then he screamed again as hard as he could. This time he was sure Buell would take off running.

Instead, the old man started to grin and held out his hand. *"Well then shake hands, mister. I married your sister!"*

## Granny's Wake

Granny Jenkins passed away some years ago. She was well up in her nineties and had lived in Greene County all her life. When she was born they found something wrong with her spine. It was bent, like a weeping willow branch, so that she spent all her days hunched over. Yet Granny lived a full life and never once complained. She eventually married a local farmer, raised some kids, sewed many beautiful quilts with the ladies at the church, and canned an untold number of jars of fruits and vegetables from her garden. She was much loved and respected throughout the community.

Out in the country, before they had funeral parlours to take care of folks, the wake would be held in someone's home. They'd often take a couple of sawboards and stretch them over the tops of two straight-back kitchen chairs. They'd place the deceased on these

101

boards covered with a long sheet. The person would be laid out like that until all the relatives and neighbors could come by and pay their respects. It was also the custom to "sit up" with the corpse throughout the night. This ancient rite derived from a superstition that spirits, or the devil, might come to steal the soul away.

Now the trouble with Granny was that she had spent more than ninety years bent over. So, when they went to place her on the boards, they couldn't get the old girl to lay flat. When they'd have her back down flush on the boards, her legs would be sticking away up in the air. Then, when they'd push her legs down, the rest of her would suddenly sit straight up. For a long while they were at a loss as to what to do with Granny. One of her sons suggested putting her in a chair in the corner and draping a blanket over her before people came by to say their farewells. But the idea was rejected. It just didn't seem respectful, was all.

Finally, Uncle Joe fashioned some rope from torn sheets he'd braided together. With the help of several strong men he managed to tie her down so she'd stay flat. When Granny was covered, no one could tell how they'd rigged her up.

All the next day folks from all over came to pay their respects. Many memories were rekindled and stories shared about her life. That night different people took turns "sitting up" with the corpse. Sometime around three o'clock in the morning, one of Granny's great grandchildren was watching the corpse. He'd gotten the job at that lonely hour because he was the youngest. He fought to stay awake until the next member of the family would take over. The boy had a small candle sitting on a stool beside him. In its yellow light, he could just make out the old woman's ghostly features. Everything else in the room was hidden in darkness and the house creaked in the dead quiet of the early hours.

It was then that the home made rope holding Granny down tore loose. Suddenly her whole body jerked upwards to a sitting position, swaying back and forth. The boy just stared wide-eyed with his hair standing on end. As he slipped off the chair and made for the door, he said over his shoulder, *"Reckon if you're the one who's going to 'sit up', I'm a-goin' to bed!"*

### The First Date

A girl's first date is something she looks forward to with great anticipation. There was a young girl who lived in Ruff Creek who'd been asked out by a local boy. She was getting ready for her date when her mother said, "Jean, honey, I want to tell you what's going to happen tonight. Roy will probably take you to a movie and, afterwards, he'll take you to an ice cream parlour. On the way home, he'll look at his watch and mention it's still early and he'll ask if you want to go for a ride. You'll say that would be nice. Then he'll take you to the top of the hill on Route 19 and turn down a gravel lane to a place called, 'Paradise Point'. After he turns off the car and switches off the lights, he'll put his arm around you. And that's when I start worrying!"

Jean listened carefully to everything her mother said. The next morning at breakfast, the young girl remarked, "Mama, I can't believe how smart you are! Everything happened last night exactly like you said it would. We went to see a Clint Eastwood movie and then Roy took me to Waynesburg for an ice cream. I had a sundae and Roy had a banana split. Then we started home and he said it was still early and would I like to drive around awhile. We went up to 'Paradise Point', just like you said. He turned off the engine and switched off the lights. Then I put my arm around him. *Let his mother do the worrying."*

## The Calf and the College Boy

There was a farmer in Ruff Creek named Paris Burton who raised beef cattle. Every spring he brought his cows down to a field close by the barn where he could keep an eye on them as they dropped their calves. One spring, a few years back, when he went to gather up his stock, he found, as in the bible story, one cow missing. He searched for a long time and finally located her at the farthest corner of his property. The poor cow was down on her side, trying to deliver her calf. She was having trouble because the calf was breach, coming out south-end first. Only the hind legs of the calf were out and the farmer couldn't pull it the rest of the way, no matter how hard he tried. The old cow was rolling her eyes and the farmer knew something had to be done quick or he'd lose mother and calf both. There wasn't time to run to the house and call the vet. The old man was desperate, trying to think of what to do.
Just then he heard a car coming down the narrow dirt road nearby. Paris climbed over the fence in time to flag it down. It was a brand-new Corvette, a metallic blue color with red racing stripes. It stopped and the biggest young man Paris had ever seen got out. The

young fellow didn't seem to have any neck at all, just a set of enormous shoulders with his head set on top like a pumpkin on a table. He was wearing a sweater that said across the front in big yellow letters, PENN STATE. Paris figured he was one of those college football players and knew his prayers had been answered!

"Sorry to bother you, son," said the old farmer, "but I've got a cow down and I'm having trouble trying to pull a calf. Do you think you could give me a hand?"

"Why, sure," replied the young fellow cheerfully. "I'd be glad to help."

They went down to the cow and Paris said, "Now, you take hold of one of the calf's legs and I'll take the other. Maybe together, we can pull it free."

However, the college boy said, "Let me give it a try on my own first." Paris agreed and the boy reached down and grabbed the calf's legs with his big strong hands and gave a little tug. Out popped the calf!

As Paris began to thank the young man, he was relieved to see the cow get back on her feet and the little calf begin to suck. It'd been a close call and the farmer gladly offered the boy a $20 bill for his trouble.

"No, that's O.K.," said the boy, refusing to take the money. "My folks taught me always to help anyone in need and not expect to get paid for it."

Paris, who was surprised to come across such a fine young person nowadays, asked if there was something else he could do for him. "You saved me hundreds of dollars," he said as they walked back to the Corvette.

As the young man opened the door of the car, he seemed to reconsider and said to Paris, "There is something you could do for me, after all. Answer a question for me. Tell me, *how fast was that calf going when it hit that cow?*"

## The New Clock

A couple lived on Bates Run back in the old days. Their names were Lee and Wiladeen Springer and one of their life's ambitions had always been to own a fancy floor clock that would strike the hour. Wiladeen saved whatever egg money she got and put it in a tin box that they kept hidden in the root cellar. Lee would add whatever extra cash he made from selling ginseng that he'd dug up in the woods. Eventually their saving paid off. They had enough money to purchase the clock.

One Saturday they went down to the jewelry store in Morgantown and picked out a tall 7-day clock in a walnut case. It would chime the hour as well as show the phases of the moon. Lee hauled it back home in his wagon and carried it up into the house. They set the clock in the corner of the front room where anyone who came in could admire it. Then Lee wound it with great care and set the long delicate hands on the correct time. A few minutes later the clock chimed! What a lovely sound it made. The couple was delighted and just sat in the room and waited for it to sound again. Each hour the beautiful clock would strike and it filled Lee and Wiladeen with warm satisfaction.

At last it got dark and was time for bed. But neither one of them wanted to leave the clock. They thought it would be a shame if the clock should chime and there wasn't anyone in the room to appreciate it. They finally agreed to take turns staying up to hear the clock. Lee said he'd sit up the first night and Wiladeen could take the following night.

Lee sat in the front room and listened to the clock

chime ten o'clock and, then, eleven o'clock. When midnight arrived, however, the clock struck twelve times but continued right on striking, 13, 14, 15, 16, without stopping. Lee ran up to the bedroom and shook his wife awake.

"Get up, Wiladeen, we've got to get out of here!" he said excitedly, *"It's later than it's ever been before!"*

## *A Ruff Encounter*

Grandpa Haniel lived up Mud Lick near Sycamore back in the days when there were very few automobiles in Greene County. In fact, the very first time Haniel ever saw one, it caused quite a stir. A lawyer in Waynesburg had purchased one of the new horseless-carriages, called an Aperson-Jackrabbit, and was taking it for a Sunday drive through the country. Haniel and his wife, Bea, were sitting on their porch when they caught sight of the odd contraption lumbering up the holler. They'd never seen anything like it before. It was banging and smoking and wheezing and it scared the old couple near to death. They both ran into the house and the old woman went and hid under the bed. She shook so hard the bed slats rattled. For his part, Haniel grabbed his shotgun from off the wall and stepped back out onto the porch again. Then, as the car came even with the house, he opened up with both barrels. The poor lawyer jumped out of the car and ran up into the woods, leaving the car to go on by itself up the road. Then slowly Bea pushed open the front door."Well, pa did you kill it?", she wanted to know.

"No," said the old man, *"but I sure made it turn loose the man it was carrying!"*

107

# CHAPTER SEVEN

# Touch of the Supernatural

*There are more things in heaven and earth, Horatio, than are dreamt of in your philosophy.* - Shakespeare

## *The Haunted Wagon*

When the miner's union first came into southwestern Pennsylvania to organize the coal miners, it often met with fierce resistance from the mine owners. One such incident involved a young, hot-blooded Irishman named Tim McGuire. He'd come to a small "coal patch", a town built and owned by a mine company, called Chelmsburg and had taken a job in the mines as a coal loader. It was a tough life for the miners and difficult to eke out a living for their families. Conditions in the early mines were treacherous. The air was bad, full of explosive black coal dust and deadly methane. Serious accidents were commonplace. Since wages were figured by the ton, an added hardship for the miners was getting honest weight from the Company for the coal dug. The Union attempted to address these conditions by organizing the miners but many of them were reluctant to get involved for fear of reprisals.

Over time, McGuire got more and more active in the Union's efforts. "I'm a Union man, first and last!" he'd brag. It wasn't long before he was branded a trouble-maker and was fired. But Tim was determined to see the mine unionized no matter what. He stayed on in the area and spent his days and nights visiting the different families of the patch and preaching the gospel of "strength through unity." Threats were made against his life but he ignored them. Once, at an organizing rally, he said he knew the mine operators wanted him run out of the coal fields or worse.

"Well, I've just got one thing to say to you, and to them parasites," he declared indignantly. "They can even try and kill me, if they've a mind to. Won't do 'em no good. The day the Company owns our lives and sweat are over. I swear before heaven, I'll not leave off until this mine lets in the union!"

Only two days later Tim McGuire was found murdered. His body was discovered by a peddler in a ditch next to the road, a mile or so from town. He'd been shot once through the forehead with a large caliber gun and his wallet was missing. The authorities determined it was a simple case of robbery but most folks allowed that Company officials had had a hand in it. It was decided to have McGuire's funeral in the evening so that the miners could attend. A large crowd showed up. Young Tim had captured both the respect and love of the close-knit community  by his defiance and courage in bucking the bosses. It was a closed-coffin ritual because the young man's face was terribly disfigured by the gunshot wound.

After the service several miners carried the coffin outside and placed it in the back of a large wagon hitched to a stout black horse. The wagon belonged to a local farmer named Ezra Smith. Ezra was standing in front of the animal, holding the bridle, as the coffin was loaded. Suddenly the horse began to act up, stamping its hooves and shaking back its powerful head. The farmer tried to calm the animal, but it was no use. The horse's nostrils flared and his white eyes rolled wild with fear. He suddenly lurched forward, knocking the old man to the ground, and galloped down the street, pulling the heavy wagon behind him.

Down the dark and empty gravel street of the coal patch the wagon rumbled, making a terrific racket, as it rocked from side to side. Sparks shot from the iron clad wheels and the horse's shoes as it careened past the Company store and school. It passed several more

111

homes without slowing until it came to a sharp turn in the road in front of the mine superintendent's house. As the terrified horse made the turn, the wagon broke loose and overturned, breaking apart and spilling the coffin on the ground. The superintendent had heard the crash and hurried outside into the dark night carrying a kerosene lamp. Holding the light out in front of him, he looked down to see the wooden coffin with the lid burst open. Staring up at him, with eyes wide, cold and lifeless, with the gruesome bullet wound in his forehead, was the face of Tim McGuire.

Soon the men chasing the wagon arrived. They hastily placed the lid back on the coffin and, hefting it up on their shoulders, carried it the remaining distance to the graveyard. The Irishman was buried in silence and a small plain stone was placed to mark his grave.

The sad events of that night were not soon forgotten in Chelmsburg. Every night thereafter the people of the patch heard with horror the sound of a runaway wagon rattling down the main street, as it had done on the night of the funeral. The distinct sound of thundering hooves and turning wheels echoed down the empty streets and even the sparks from the iron horseshoes could be seen. Folks hid behind their locked doors and drawn shades. No other sound could be heard in the town but the creaking of the haunted wagon.

This went on for over three years, night after night, as a continual reminder of McGuire's death and his fateful promise. Then a day arrived when the dreadful wagon was heard no more. For on that very same day, after years of struggle and faith, the United Mine Workers Union was voted into the coal mine. The people of Chelmsburg figured McGuire had seen his wish fulfilled and had at last gone to his eternal rest.

## *An Incident on Opening Day*

Back in early 1975, a couple from Pittsburgh moved to Greene County and purchased a small farm near Sycamore. Dan and Cindy Loughton were fed up with dealing with urban life and its continual traffic noise, sulphur-tainted air, and constant stress. They felt that the city was no place to raise a family. They both made their livings as writers and didn't have to live in town. So when Cindy found out she was pregnant, they packed up their typewriters and left for the country.

It was springtime when they moved into their new home and Dan started going to the auctions held around the county. He needed to purchase a number of things to equip their farm and, as a writer, he thoroughly enjoyed observing the colorful characters who attended these sales. Dan and Cindy were quiet folks and, as their work kept them at home most of the time, they didn't reach out and become part of the community. The local people, for their part, left the couple alone. Had things been different, in this regard, what happened later may have been prevented.

One evening Dan was at an auction being held at the fairgrounds in Waynesburg. A number of items were consigned to be sold that night and, in looking them over, Dan saw several tools and an old-fashioned ice cream freezer he wanted. Something else that caught his eye was a hunting rifle. His father was a gun collector and Dan had learned a good deal about the subject from him while growing up. He recognized the rifle as a World War II German Mauser refitted with a custom walnut stock. It was in excellent shape with good rifling and a snug-fitting bolt. Inlaid under the forearm

113

was an oval silver plate with the initials "L.H." engraved on it. Dan assumed the rifle would fetch a high price and, as they were low on money after the move, he resolved not to even bid on it.

Soon afterwards the hunting rifle was put up for sale but the auctioneer had trouble getting the bidding underway. He started off at $200, and then came down to $150, but was still unsuccessful.

Finally he said, "Come on, folks, don't let this pretty rifle go by. Who'll start the bidding at $100, do I have $100? anyone $100?"

On the spur of the moment Dan yelled out, "$75!"

The auctioneer picked it up and called out, "I've got $75 on this fine rifle, who'll make it $85? do I hear $85?" But there was no response. No one seemed to show any interest. "Sold!" said the auctioneer, banging down the gavel.

Dan held up his number and one the assistants brought the rifle over to him. Most times, when someone gets a good buy at an auction, the folks sitting around the successful bidder will smile or nod. Dan, on the other hand, had an uneasy sense that no one wanted to even look at him. It was unsettling somehow but the feeling soon passed as the night wore on and he bid on other items. He finally took his newly-acquired purchases, stowed them in the back of his truck, and headed for home. He thought he'd either keep the rifle for himself or give it to his father for Christmas.

Life went on as usual until that fall when deer-hunting season drew near. It seemed as though everywhere Dan went, the talk was all about it. Dan hadn't decided, one way or the other, if he would do any hunting now that he lived in the country. He had

114

only hunted a few times when he was younger but he liked the taste of venison. He also felt that it was somehow more honest to kill his own meat instead of going to the supermarket for it. The week before the season opened, as he was walking past the sporting goods store in Waynesburg, he made up his mind. He went in and purchased several boxes of 8 mm shells, a bright orange safety vest, and a pair of high-top insulated boots.

Opening Day, Dan got up at five a.m.. It was still dark out but the stars were beginning to fade. Without waking his wife, he dressed warmly and drank some coffee. He took the rifle he'd bought at the auction and slipped in some shells. He then started up the hill in the dark. It was cold and his breath blew clouds of white vapor as he climbed the steep hillside. By the time he'd reached the summit the featureless night had given way to a mist-strewn grey dawn. He turned north along the ridge, keeping downwind of any deer which might be ahead of him. The trees all around were small and thick, with occasional clear patches of tall grass. The field had once been a hay meadow but was now grown up with sassafras and hickory trees. The piercing cry of a red-tailed hawk as it flew overhead made him start. The unexpected sound breaking the deep silence of the frosty morning filled Dan's heart with a strange sense of dread and foreboding. It conjured up in his mind's eye the image of wind blowing across a lonely grave. He shuddered and found he was sweating and clutching the rifle tightly in both hands.

Then as Dan stepped forward, a large buck-deer suddenly bounded from a thicket in front of him and to his right. Its white tail flashed as the fleet animal leapt

115

away through the trees. Dan was so startled that, by the time he'd raised the rifle, the deer was gone. He stood still trying to calm his nerves. He felt that the buck had not gone far and he might yet get a shot at it, if he just waited awhile. Already he could hear the echoing reports of gunshots from the hills around him. He waited half an hour. It was now clear day and the mists were burning off the higher ridges.

Dan began to move slowly forward again, this time determined not to be caught unawares. The ground began to fall slightly under him. Then, just in front, in a cluster of high brown grass and briars, there was movement. He waited, holding his breath. Then the buck's tail flashed white, giving him away. Dan's response was pure instinct. He heard the roar of the large caliber rifle before he realized he had even pulled the trigger. With a pounding heart he moved cautiously towards the deer. But what he found, instead, lying motionless among the tall grass, was the body of a young boy in a white, blood-stained jacket.

Dan staggered at the sight, it was so unexpected and so dreadful. The child's eyes were open and stared up into the blue sky. His face was colorless, like carved white stone. Dan fell to his knees besides the little boy. It was like a nightmare from which he desperately hoped to awaken. He lifted the boy's lifeless hand and, then, let it drop with a groan that was wrenched from the depths of his soul. He began to sob uncontrollably, both for the unknown boy and for himself.

Rousing himself, Dan left the corpse and stumbled back down the hillside to his home. In despair, he told his wife the awful truth of what had happened. He then called the police. Soon afterwards a police car came up to the house. Driving it was the county sheriff, Walter Brice, who had the unhappy duty of investigating the tragedy. Brice had witnessed a great deal of trouble in his time. He asked Dan to take him up to the boy. They climbed the hillside together until they came to the abandoned meadow. But the boy was not there.

With his mind reeling, Dan swore to the sheriff that it was the very spot where he'd murdered the boy.

"Some other hunters must have come along and moved his body," Dan reasoned. The sheriff asked Dan to describe the boy as best he could. "Well, he was wearing a white jacket, brown pants and boots. There was a short rifle next to him and he had red hair," answered Dan. "He couldn't of been more than 11 or 12 years old, I guess."

A disturbed look of recognition flickered across the sheriff's face and Dan asked if he knew the boy.

"No," said Brice, "it just made me think of something, that's all. But either you were seeing things, mister, or you've got the wrong place. If the boy's body had been here, like you said, the grass would be matted down and there'd be some sign of blood, most likely. But you can see nothing's been in this place for days. We'd better go back and have you fill out a report. See if we can get to the bottom of this."

They had begun to leave when Dan turned back to retrieve his rifle which he earlier had left leaning against a tree. As he came back towards the sheriff, Brice looked with keen interest at the weapon.

"Where'd you come by that rifle, anyhow?" he asked. Dan told him how he'd purchased it at the auction that spring. Brice asked to see it and then turned it over and looked at something. The sheriff suddenly dropped the rifle as if it had burned his hands.

Controlling his voice with difficulty, Brice said, "I've seen that gun before. Just last year. Belonged to Lon Harris over in Pine Bank. That's his initials on the underside." He paused awhile and then went on. "Lon went hunting on Opening Day last year and his son wanted to go with him. The boy was awfully young, 11 years old, I think, but Lon agreed to take him along anyway. The boy had a small carbine and his father gave him a stand out in the woods. He told the boy to make sure that he didn't move from the spot and to shoot if a deer came his way. Lon then went off a short ways and took a stand himself. There was a lot of shooting going on and the deer were moving around pretty good."

"Well, I reckon the boy got scared," continued Brice, "or just plain bored. Anyway, as we figured it out later, he went looking for his father. There was a good deal of thick undergrowth and when Lon saw something moving, he shot at it, thinking it was a deer. The poor child was hit and died instantly, shot through the chest. Lon went off his head afterwards, it seems. When her husband and boy didn't return home, Lon's wife, Sophie, asked some neighbors to look for them. They found Lon up in the woods. He was wandering around aimless, carrying his little boy in his arms."

The sheriff was quiet as Dan took the story in.

"I was in charge of the investigation," Brice continued. "Lon wasn't charged, everyone knew it was an accident. The family sold out and left the county soon after that. I'm afraid the rifle you bought at the auction was Lon's, the one that killed his boy."

As Dan and the sheriff turned to leave, a confusing array of questions and thoughts flooded their minds. All that had happened, all that had seemed so real, Dan now realized, had only been a terrifying apparition and nothing more. He left the haunted rifle laying on the ground among the trees where it could rust away with the passing years. Never again would the heartbreaking tragedy be reenacted. Then as the two men began to descend the hill, Dan heard once more the clear, plaintive cry of the red-tail hawk as it soared high overhead.

## The Card Game

There was a truck driver named Blackie Hensley who lived near Holbrook. He drove a large stainless-steel milk truck and his job took him all over the county collecting milk from a number of small private dairies. He was a likable fellow but not at all religious. He trusted to his own wits and courage and left the rest to chance.

One Saturday night, Blackie was sitting in on a poker game over in Rice's Landing. There were three other men in the game with a twenty dollar limit. Blackie got on a lucky streak late in the evening and was raking in the chips. It seemed as if each hand that he was dealt was better than the one before. He just couldn't lose. Finally, one of the men, a school teacher named Pete Jarvis, began to count up his few remaining chips. "Cash me in, boys," he said, looking at his watch, "it's getting on midnight, time to quit." One of the other men got up and began to stretch.

Then Blackie said, "Why, Jarvis, there's no reason to stop now. I aim to get all the rest of your money soon." But Pete insisted, saying his wife would be waiting on him.

119

"You know same as me, Pete, she'll be dead asleep." chided Blackie. "Truth is, you're just scared of losing your pocket money, ain't that right?"

The other men were having a good time and were willing to play awhile longer, but Pete said uneasily, "Well, it's not only the wife. It's the Sabbath now. It's just not right to gamble on the Lord's Day."

Blackie threw his head back and laughed. He said that he'd stopped going to Sunday School when he was a kid. Sunday to him was the same as any other day. But no matter what Blackie or the others said, Pete's mind was set. He cashed in his chips, put on his hat and coat, and said good night.

Only a few minutes had passed, when there was a knock on the door. "Knew he'd change his mind," said Blackie, grinning, as he got up and opened the door. Instead of Pete, however, there was another man, a stranger, standing in the doorway.

"What do you want, mister?" said Blackie, somewhat surprised by the man's appearance at such a late hour.

"Heard you boys have a little card game going, " the man said. "I'm just traveling through on business and would like to sit in, if you don't mind?"

Blackie looked closely at the stranger. The man didn't strike him as a policeman of any sort, so he said, "We could use a fourth, but tell us how you heard of our little game, in the first place?" The man said he'd learned of the game from over in Dry Tavern.

"Alright, come on in, mister," said Blackie. "It's an informal game we've got here and if your money's good, I'll see if I can relieve you of some of it. I'm on quite a roll right now, so take care!"

It wasn't until the stranger had entered the room that they realized how tall he was, well over six feet. His clothing was first class but he had on some kind of cologne that reeked in the smoky room. Blackie figured he must be a salesman and asked him what line he was in.

"The name is Jack," said the man in a friendly way, "Jack Tombs, from New York. I sell a little of everything and even do some buying when the price is right." He reached out his large hand to shake and Blackie caught a glint of the diamond cuff link he wore. One of the other men began to deal the cards. Blackie picked his up and was looking at a natural flush. It was his lucky night, he thought with jubilation, make no mistake!

Blackie won the next two hands but lost the third, along with a tidy sum, when he tried to outbluff the stranger. He had a queer feeling that the tall man knew exactly which cards he held in his hand. Then the stranger started to win. With each hand, their money flowed to him. No matter which game they played, five-card stud or draw, Tombs' pile of chips grew steadily before him. Hours passed without notice. Each man was completely preoccupied with the game, as if nothing else in the world mattered. Blackie's eyes smarted from the cigarette smoke which floated ghost-like in the room as he watched the stranger over his cards. He suspected the city fellow of cheating but, for the life of him, he couldn't catch him at it. He'd lost all he'd made earlier in the evening and a great deal of his own money besides.

Finally Blackie's friends said they'd had enough. They got up and put on their coats and left. Blackie was down to his last couple of dollars.

"Mister," he said, "I swear to heaven, you sure can play cards. You've done me in, and that's a fact!"   As he started to rise, the tall man looked at him and said in a soft, deep voice, "You might as well bet it all, Blackie. Who knows, you may get lucky again." There was something about the man that made Blackie uneasy. He couldn't quite put his finger on it. For one thing, he didn't care for the way the man said his name, like he'd known him for a long time. Yet the man's words stirred something in him. A wild crazy hope of recouping his losses with one last hand suddenly seized Blackie with a sort of recklessness.

Pulling a blank check from his wallet, he said, "Alright, Mr. Tombs, let's see what you're made of. One last hand to finish the night, no limit. You agree?"

The stranger smiled and began shuffling the cards in his smooth large hands with a slow rhythm. After pushing the deck across the table for Blackie to cut, he began to deal a hand of five-card draw. Blackie picked up his cards and saw four queens staring back at him. His fatigue and caution disappeared. He knew he was going to win.

"Mister, will you accept my check? Seems you're the only one with money around here. If not, I'll put this watch up," said Blackie, unfastening his watch from his wrist. He was desperate to up the bet.

Tombs smiled and said, "Just hold on to your check and wristwatch, Blackie. The only bet I'll take is your I.O.U. and we'll settle up later."

Blackie, sure he would win, hastily agreed. Holding on to his queens, he threw away a nine. When the man dealt him another card, however, it slid off the green felt table down onto the floor. Blackie leaned over to pick it up and happened to see from under the table that the stranger had slipped off his fancy leather boots.

There, instead of human feet, he saw two cloven hooves! With blinding certainty, Blackie realized that he had been playing cards with none other than the Devil himself!

In sudden panic, Blackie jerked upward, catching the end of the table with his shoulder and upsetting it. Cards and money spilled over the floor. With no thought but to get away, Blackie bolted for the door. Ice cold fear swept through him as he bounded down the steps into the cold light of morning. He ran down the empty street without once looking back.

Later, when he'd recovered, he told his friends the dreadful tale. "I know," said Blackie, in earnest, "that if he had won my I.O.U., I would have been lost for all time. It's by the grace of God that I escaped."

Blackie Hensley had learned his lesson. He never played cards on the Sabbath again. Or on any other day, for that matter!

### The Message

Sometime in the 1920's, there were two brothers who were partners in a small coal mine in Greene County. Their names were Leyland and James Matthews and they called their operation the "Red Star Mine". James was an engineer and responsible for the mine's day-to-day operation, while his older brother, Leyland, handled the financial and sales end of the business. The men who worked in the coal fields in the early days were a rough bunch and the two brothers were no exception. Even though their operation was quite successful, there were often bitter disputes between them. Often the cause of the strife was insignificant but their

123

tempers would rise, nonetheless, like methane gas filling a mine shaft, until there'd be a spark, an accusation or insult, and there'd be an explosion. Usually these violent arguments would take place behind closed doors in the office or down at the mine. Once, however, they got into fisticuffs in the restaurant of the Fort Jackson Hotel in Waynesburg and broke up the place. A table-full of dishes and several chairs were destroyed in the ruckus and the police had to be called in. The brothers didn't speak to each other for days afterwards. Then one day Leyland let it be known that the brothers had dissolved the partnership. He said he'd bought out James' share of the Red Star and his younger brother had gone out west someplace to try his hand at hard-rock mining. It was common knowledge that Leyland had withdrawn a considerable amount of cash money from the bank to pay his brother off. Most folks in Greene County were not surprised by the break-up and said it was long overdue. A few, however, wondered at the suddenness of it all and why the younger Matthews hadn't bothered to say goodbye to anyone. Things settled down after that and, as Leyland's ventures prospered, he opened several more mines in the area and a trucking operation. He moved into a large house in Waynesburg and became one of the pillars of the community.

Some thirty years later, in the mid-1950's, a new small mine opened up near Ruff Creek. It was a busy time in the coal fields then with numerous mines working. The operation only involved one Continuous Miner, a new mining machine recently introduced into the industry, and a crew of men to work it. Every couple of days or so, after the miners had completed their shift, an engineer would go down into the mine with his maps and transit and set the points for the next day's work. He'd leave whatever instructions and corrections were needed on a slate board at the mine face for the foreman to read in the morning.

One morning, however, when the foreman, Gale Darney, started his shift, he found unexpected instructions on the slate board. Written in white chalk on the blackboard were the words, *turn bearing 64° left and continue.*

Darney was surprised by the radical change in direction of the shaft called for in the new instructions but he reset his equipment and began work. He was further puzzled as the width of the seam diminished the farther they mined in the new direction. He was tempted to shut down and go aboveground to verify the instructions. This would take a considerable amount of time, however, and would mean lost revenues. He resigned himself to keep going until the end of the shift and check it out afterwards.

The Continuous Miner made a deafening roar as it spit pieces of black coal and slate, sending them to the surface on the snake-like conveyor. Suddenly, without warning, the face gave way into an open, black hole. Darney pushed the lever to shut down the machine and, in the silence that followed, he climbed forward and into the opening. They apparently had broken through into some old abandoned mine workings. Darney knew from experience that they had been lucky. If the old mine had been filled with water, which was often the case, they might all have drowned. But there was still danger. The foreman immediately took his safety lamp from his belt and tested for gas. The air was safe. Darney then went on to check out the old mine, continually testing for gas. In the near total darkness, the light from his carbide lamp shown on the wet green moss which clung like ivy to the mine's old wooden ribs and roof supports. Everywhere there was the sound of dripping water, adding to the sense of loneliness and gloom that permeated the place. It was like an old underground tomb that had been sealed against invasion from ancient times.

The foreman traversed one passage and then turned down another. A few feet further on he came to a stop. Although the underground temperature remains constant, Darney distinctly felt a cold draft that chilled him to the bone. He peered into the blackness, straining his eyes, reluctant, for some reason, to go any further. It was then that Darney saw a dead man lying on the rock floor a few feet ahead of him.

There was no way to tell how long the man had been there. His skull and the bones of his hands glowed white in the foreman's light and his clothing had rotted away in places. He wasn't dressed like a working miner, although he wore a miners hat and old-fashioned light. There was a wooden equipment box next to him, similar to the ones used by engineers for their instruments. Stenciled on the side of the box were the words, "Red Star Mine".

Work was called off for the day and the mine owner, after hearing Darney's story, reported the discovery to the authorities. An investigation was carried out and the dead man was identified as James Matthews. The cause of death was a fractured skull caused by a sharp blow to the head. No money was found on the deceased. Although a clear case of murder, and probable robbery, no one was ever charged. The older brother when questioned claimed complete ignorance of how his brother came to be in the mine. Leyland swore he'd seen his brother off at the train station and had never heard from him again. But the people of Greene County believed differently.

Soon afterwards, feeling the accusing eyes of the community upon him, Leyland sold his house and business interests and moved to Pittsburgh. He died there a few years later, quite wealthy, but without family or friends with him when the end came.

Not long after Darney had found the corpse, he was talking with the engineer. "It's quite a coincidence that we stumbled on that old mine and cleared up the matter of Matthew's disappearance. Still, I can't rightly understand why you had us change our bearings 64° like that in the first place?"

The engineer, a young man from West Virginia, looked at the foreman with bewilderment. "I don't know what you're talking about. I wasn't even in the mine the night before you fellows started that shift. And I certainly wouldn't have had you leave the main part of the seam like that and go off the wrong way."

Darney said the instructions were written on the board, plain as day, so he followed them.

"Well, I have no idea who wrote those instructions, Darney," said the engineer, "but I assure you, it sure wasn't me!"

# CHAPTER EIGHT

# At the Gates of Heaven

*A pious friend inquired of Henry Thoreau, "Have you made your peace with God?" Thoreau replied, "No, we have never quarrelled."*

## The Steel Company President

Times have been difficult for the steel industry in western Pennsylvania in recent years with many of the large steel mills closing down and people out of work. Whenever steel is down, coal mining suffers as well. The president of a large steel company up in Pittsburgh passed away recently. He arrived at the gates of heaven but, when he asked for admittance, he received an unexpected reply.

"Why, you're welcome in heaven, Mr. Brodlick," said St. Peter, "especially since you donated all that money to your church building fund. But the truth is, we've been having sort of a problem up here lately with housing. You see, ever since those T.V. evangelists started up, there's been so many 'saved' souls pouring in that we're nearly over-run. Now I admit, there's been a drop from that source lately, but we still haven't quite caught up yet. There's a new building that's just about completed, we're going to call it the "Celestial Condominiums", and it'll be ready next week. If you'd help us out and go down to hell for one week, we'll call you when it's finished. You can have your choice of rooms then, how about it?"

The steel president thought he could handle hell for a little while. Afterall, he'd be in heaven for eternity, what was one little week in hell compared with that?"

So he agreed and St. Peter sent him on his way. About four days later, however, the phone was ringing off the hook. It was the Devil calling St. Peter.

"Whatever you do, St. Peter," said the Devil, in great agitation, "come down here and get that fellow. *He's closed three furnaces down here already!*"

130

### The Taxi Driver and the Preachers

There was a taxi driver named Elwood Perkins who worked for a cab company in Waynesburg. He drove a big, eight-cylinder Ford L.T.D. painted green and white and he'd burn up the winding roads of Greene County taking folks to the doctor's office or shopping at the I.G.A..

One time he had to drive all the way to the airport in Pittsburgh to collect two ministers who were coming to Waynesburg for a big revival meeting. They were both nationally-known evangelists and there were banners up all over town advertising their arrival. Elwood and his passengers were barreling down the interstate near Bridgeville when a big eighteen-wheeler just in front of them blew a front tire and jackknifed in the middle of the highway. They ran smack into the truck and all three men were killed instantly.

They soon showed up at the gates of heaven where St. Peter was waiting to greet them. He swung open the Pearly Gates and motioned for the taxi driver to go in first, followed by the ministers. They strolled along the golden streets with St. Peter showing them the sights. Everything was so clean and shiny. When they finally came to the Heavenly Harp factory, they went in and St. Peter told Elwood to pick out the harp he wanted. When he'd made his choice, St. Peter then directed the ministers to choose the harps they wanted.

They then continued along until they turned up the drive to Moses Mansions. Again St. Peter asked Elwood to choose which of the houses he wanted to live in. Each house was different and Elwood looked them over a good bit before deciding. He finally asked

131

for the big, two-story house at the end. Only then were the ministers asked to choose the ones they wanted.

At last one of the ministers, the one with the higher television rating, spoke up.

"Excuse me, St. Peter," he said, in a respectful way, "but there's something here I don't quite understand. My colleague and I have dedicated our entire lives to preaching and saving souls and yet this taxi driver seems to be getting preferential treatment. I'm not complaining for myself, you understand, but it just doesn't seem fair."

"I know that you fellows have saved many souls and we here in heaven are most grateful," St. Peter said to the minister. "But you see, this taxi driver deserves special treatment. *Why, he's scared the hell out of more people than all of your preaching combined!*"

## The Nervous Man

Some folks try to reach the gates of heaven without waiting for nature to take its course. There was a fellow living in Ruff Creek one time whose name was Cleve Mumford and he was one of the most naturally nervous people that ever lived. He was always worrying that things wouldn't work out and most of the time, for him, they didn't. He was constantly fussing to make extra sure that whatever he was doing worked out right. It drove most folks who knew him to distraction. His wife, one day, had had enough. She packed up the kids, left a note, and cleared out.

The very next day, Cleve's boss called him into the office and gave him his walking papers. "You're a nice enough fellow, Mumford," he said, "but the truth is, I

132

can't afford to keep you on. You take such pains getting things done the way you figure they should be, I'm losing money. It takes you four times longer to finish a job of work than anybody else."

Cleve returned home to find a letter from the I.R.S. informing him that there was a problem with his last tax return. He'd reworked it over fourteen times and now he was going to be audited. This was the final humiliation and he decided the only thing left for him to do was to commit suicide.

Cleve went down to the general store and asked Ray if he had any rope that a man could use to hang himself. Ray went in the back and cut him a ten-foot section of stout manila rope. Laying it on the counter, he asked pleasantly, "Will there be anything else, Cleve?" The nervous man got to thinking he'd better have a back-up of some kind.

He asked, "What's that revolver you have in the case there?" Ray took it out and let him look it over. It was a .38-special Smith and Wesson. Cleve went ahead and purchased it, along with a box of shells. But he was still worried about getting the job done right.

"How about some strong poison, you got any?" After searching around in the storeroom, Ray found a box of rat-poison. It had skull and cross-bone warnings all over it and looked potent enough to kill all the Democrats in Ruff Creek. But Cleve was still fretting about his suicide, so he asked Ray to sell him a gallon of kerosene and a box of kitchen matches so he could burn himself up as well.

Finally even Cleve was satisfied that he had enough deadly paraphernalia to get the job done right. Late that night, just after midnight, he drove over to the Masontown bridge. It's a high bridge over the

Monongahalia River between Greene and Fayette
counties. There wasn't any traffic at that hour to inter-
fere with his plans. He went out to the middle of the
bridge and tied one end of the thick rope to the railing.
The other end of the rope he fashioned into a hang-
man's noose like the ones he'd seen on T.V. westerns.
He smeared it with lard, so it would slide easy. He put
his head through the noose and tightened it around
his neck. He'd already soaked his clothing in kerosene.
To finish up he gulped down the evil-tasting poison
and pulled the loaded pistol from his belt. He climbed
up on the railing, with the revolver in one hand and a
match in the other. It was Cleve's moment of truth.
But, instead of thinking about his past or what might
be on the other side, Cleve was still concerned that
everything go right with his suicide. Finally he struck
the match and set himself on fire. He then jumped off
the bridge and, at the same time, put the gun to his
head. The trouble was, he reached the end of the rope
as he pulled the trigger and it jerked his hand up. The
.38 slug just missed his head and cut the rope. He fell
down into the river, which put the fire out. He then
drank so much of the dirty river water that he threw
up all the poison. And it was a mighty good thing
Cleve knew how to swim, *or he'd of drowned for sure!*

### Kissy's Dream

One morning Kissy came into the general store and
started telling Ray and some of the others about a
dream he'd had that night.
"I dreamt I'd died and went down to the place below,"
he said. "I was walking along with the Devil himself

when we came to a door. The Devil opened it and I saw a small room with Howard Hughes sitting inside on a chair. Then another door opened and a huge, old she-gorilla came in and sat down next to him. She had long, dirty fur hanging down all over and stank to high heavens. I asked the Devil what was going on and he said that Mr. Hughes hadn't led a very good life. Now he had to spend eternity with the gorilla as his punishment."

"We walked on down to another door and opened it. There was William Casey of the C.I.A. sitting on a chair. Then a door over on the side opened and another she-gorilla came in. She was even uglier, and smelled worse, than the first one. She put her long hairy arms around the poor man and started hugging him and kissing him on the side of his face. It was horrible. I looked at the Devil and he nodded. He said that Casey hadn't led a very good life and now he had to stay with the gorilla for all time."

At this point, Kissy took a break in his story to pour some coffee.

"Well, what happened next?" the fellows all wanted to know.

"Now that's the sad part," went on Kissy, with a sigh. "Me and the Devil come to another room and went in. And there was Ray Stockdale sitting on a chair all by himself. Then a door comes open and Marilyn Monroe walks in and sits down next to him! She was beautiful, just like her pictures. I said to the Devil that there must be some kind of mistake. I told him I'd known Ray for a long time and that he couldn't deserve a woman as pretty as that."

'You don't understand, Kissy.' the Devil told me. 'You see, *Marilyn didn't lead a very good life!*'."

135